An Introduction
3D MicroStation 95

An Introduction to 3D MicroStation 95

A. Yarwood

 LONGMAN

Addison Wesley Longman Limited
Edinburgh Gate, Harlow
Essex CM20 2JE, England
and Associated Companies throughout the world

© Addison Wesley Longman Limited 1997

First published 1997

British Library Cataloguing in Publication Data
A catalogue entry for this title is available from the British Library

ISBN 0-582-30708-2

Set by 24 in 10/13pt Melior
Produced by Longman Singapore Publishers (Pte) Ltd
Printed in Singapore

Contents

List of plates

Colour plates are between pages 98 and 99.

Preface

MicroStation 95 is a first class computer aided design (CAD) software package in worldwide use. Its use is particularly strong in the architectural profession. MicroStation 95 is available in versions to run under Dos, Windows 3.1x, Windows 95 and Windows NT. It is also available for the Mac OS and other platforms.

In addition to being able to use the software for the construction of 2D (two-dimensional) technical drawings as described in my earlier book *An Introduction to MicroStation 95*, the software contains a group of tools for the construction of 3D solid model drawings. In addition to the 3D tools native to MicroStation 95, an add-on software package, MicroStation Modeler, can be loaded to work in MicroStation 95 giving another group of 3D tools, implementing those native to MicroStation 95. Three chapters introduce the use of MicroStation Modeler.

MicroStation 95 is an extremely complex programme. The addition of MicroStation Modeler adds a further complexity making it quite impossible to describe all the possible methods of constructing 3D models with the aid of two software packages in a book of this size. It is, however, hoped that this introductory text will encourage students and those commencing to learn how to use the software for the construction of 3D models to get to grips with the software and so be encouraged to continue learning how to use MicroStation 95 with the aim of becoming expert in its use.

When the book was first envisaged, it was hoped to include a chapter or two on the use of MicroStation Masterpiece, which is another MicroStation add-on package designed for the rendering of 3D solid model drawings constructed within MicroStation and Modeler. In order to allow the book to be published at a price suitable for students and other beginners, I have found it impossible to include an introduction to Masterpiece. MicroStation Masterpiece is, however, a rendering package which takes rendering beyond the facilities available in MicroStation itself.

The contents of the book form a course of work covering the essentials for constructing 3D Models in MicroStation 95. The emphasis on the examples given throughout the book is on mechanical engineering and general technical drawing, despite the fact that the use of the software is strong in the architectural professions. Its contents form a course of work suitable for students requiring to learn CAD when undertaking vocational courses, City & Guilds and mechanical engineering first-year courses in universities which involve the use of CAD. Students and their teachers in sixth forms of secondary schools who are taking CAD as part of technology courses may also find the book to be of value. The book should also be suitable for those new to and wishing to learn CAD methods involving MicroStation 95 in industry.

An eight-page full-colour section containing 16 colour plates is included to show the use of colour when constructing 3D models with the aid of MicroStation 95 and its add-on MicroStation Modeler. The colour section shows renderings of 3D models which have been used as examples in the book.

The book's contents are based on the use of the software as loaded on a personal computer (PC) running Windows 95. Its contents are quite suitable for those working with the DOS version of the software and are also applicable to MicroStation 95 operating on other platforms.

A. Yarwood
Salisbury 1997

Acknowledgements

Trademarks

MicroStation® is a registered trademark, and the following are trademarks, of Bentley Systems, Inc.:

MicroStation Modeler™, MicroStation Masterpiece™

IBM® is a registered trademark of International Business Machines Corporation.

Windows™ is a trademark, and MS-DOS® is a registered trademark, of Microsoft Corporation.

CHAPTER 1

Introduction

This book has been written as an introduction to pupils in schools, students in colleges and other beginners who wish to learn how to construct 3D solid model drawings with the aid of the computer-aided design (CAD) software package **MicroStation 95**. The book has been compiled on the assumption that the reader is already capable of using the software to construct 2D technical drawings. To fully describe how to work with a complex CAD system such as MicroStation 95 would require a book considerably larger than this one. It is hoped however that readers of this book will be encouraged to use MicroStation 95 and once introduced to constructing 3D model drawings with its aid, become sufficiently interested to go on to learn more about how to use the software to construct more complex 3D models.

The software can be installed to run under MS-DOS, Windows 95 or Windows NT. This book is concerned specifically with the Windows 95 version; however, the DOS and NT versions are sufficiently similar to enable the operator to work from the descriptions contained in this book. Also, although the contents of the book are suitable for use with the software working on other platforms, we are only concerned here with operation on a fully IBM-compatible personal computer (PC).

Hardware requirements

Operating chip: At least an Intel (or similar) 80836 chip or better. If an 80836 or an 80846SX, then a math coprocessor chip must also be fitted. If an 80846DX, then the math coprocessor chip is integral to the operating chip. If a Pentium (or similar) operating chip is fitted, faster working will be possible.

Hard disk size: At least 30 Mbytes free space, preferably more. MicroStation files require a minimum of 14 Mbytes, with a maximum of 70 Mbytes – depending upon the type of installation required. A further 15 Mbytes of disk space is required when running the software.

Random access memory (RAM): At least 8 Mbytes of RAM are required, but 16 Mbytes will allow for larger drawing files and faster operation. The amount of RAM required basically depends upon the size of the drawing. As far as the drawings described in this book are concerned it would be best to have 16 Mbytes RAM.

Digitiser: This book deals only with a Microsoft compatible mouse with two buttons – a *left* button and a *right* button. MicroStation can be worked with the aid of a three-button mouse or a digitising tablet and puck, but their use is not described here.

Visual display unit: All work described here will be based upon the use of a single VDU (monitor or screen), although two VDUs can be fitted – one for graphics, the other for alphanumeric (text and figures) information. It is advisable for the VDU to be at least SVGA standard (at least 800 by 600 pixels). In all graphics work such as CAD, the bigger the VDU screen the better. Although one can work with a 14 inch screen, a 15 inch, 17 inch or larger screen is advisable. The problem, however, is cost. Screens larger than 14 inch are considerably more expensive.

Terms used throughout this book

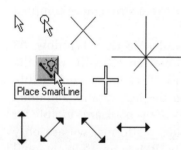

Fig. 1.1 The types of cursor used in MicroStation 95

As stated earlier, a two-button mouse is used for all operations described in this book. The mouse may also be used at times in conjunction with the computer keyboard. The following terms are used to describe frequently performed operations when working in MicroStation:

Cursor: A variety of cursors of different shapes are employed in working both Windows 95 and MicroStation 95. Some of these are shown in Fig. 1.1.

Enter: Type the letters, figures or word(s) that follow at the keyboard.

Key-in: *enter* names or abbreviations in the **Key in** window.

Left-click: Press the left-hand button of the mouse. In MicroStation 95 manuals you will see this referred to at times as a *data point*.

Right-click: Press the right-hand button of the mouse.

Drag: Position the cursor under mouse control over the feature to be *dragged*. Press and hold down the mouse button. Move the mouse and the feature will move in response.

Double-click: Press a mouse button twice in quick succession.

Both-click: Press both buttons of the mouse at the same time. In MicroStation 95 Manuals you will see this referred to for some operations as a *tentative point*.

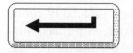

Fig. 1.2 The arrow type **Return** or **Enter** key of a computer keyboard

Return: Press the **Return** key of the keyboard. This key is often marked with **Enter** instead of **Return**, or may have an arrow as shown in Fig. 1.2.

Fig 1.3 The **Main** tool box

Fig. 1.4 The **Linear Elements** flyout

Fig. 1.5 The **Place Circle by Center** tool tip

Tool box: This is a set of tool icons within a box – Fig. 1.3 shows the **Main** tool box.

Flyout: When an outward pointing arrow is seen in the right-hand bottom corner of a tool icon in a tool box, holding down a *left-click* on the icon a *flyout* showing a palette in line with the icon appears. Figure 1.4 shows the **Linear Elements** flyout.

Tool tip: When the cursor, under mouse control, is placed over a tool icon, the name of the tool represented by the icon appears as a tool tip. Figure 1.5 shows the tool tip for the **Place Circle by Center** tool icon.

Element: This is a feature drawn in MicroStation with the aid of a tool. Figure 1.6 shows some typical elements. Note, however, that some elements may consist of several, when in a block or a group.

Highlight: This is a feature that changes its colours and background. Examples are shown in Figs 1.3 and 1.4 in which tool icons have been selected by a *left-click* on the icons. The icon colour reverses from black to white and the background reverses from grey to black.

A design file for personal use

Most of the drawings contained as illustrations in this book are constructed in the personal design file described in this chapter. I have saved this design file on my computer as **ay.dgn** – my initials (ay) followed by the filename extension *.dgn. In order to follow the methods of construction described in future pages, it is advisable to construct a similar personal design file of your own.

You may find settings, other than those given here, to be more suitable for your own methods of construction in MicroStation 95. If you are at all unsure, it may be best to set up a personal design file as described below. In any case it is advisable to experiment with a variety of settings to familiarise yourself with the available possibilities.

Stages in constructing the personal design file

Stage 1

1. Start up MicroStation 95 from the Windows 95 Start-up window. In the **MicroStation Manager** dialogue box which appears, select **Status Bar** from the **Style:** box. Then select the directory

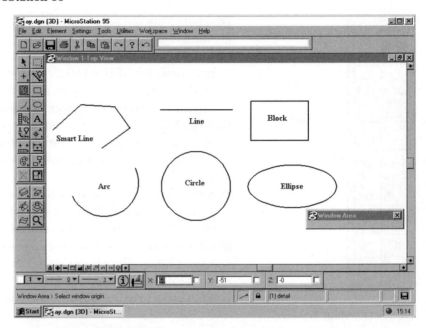

Fig. 1.6 MicroStation 95
elements

dgn\mechdft from the ustation directory list. In the file list,
double-click on the filename **a3form.dgn** (Fig. 1.7). This design file
will be the basis for our personal file.

2. The **a3form.dgn** design screen appears as shown in Fig. 1.8. The
drawing shows a border and title block, which we will not be using.

Stage 2

1. As a precautionary measure, in the **File** pull-down menu *left-click*
on **Save As...** and save the file to the name **ay.dgn** as in Fig. 1.9.

Fig. 1.7 *Left-click* on the
filename **a3form.dgn** in the
MicroStation Manager
dialogue box

Fig. 1.8 The **a3form.dgn** screen for **ay.dgn** as it first appears

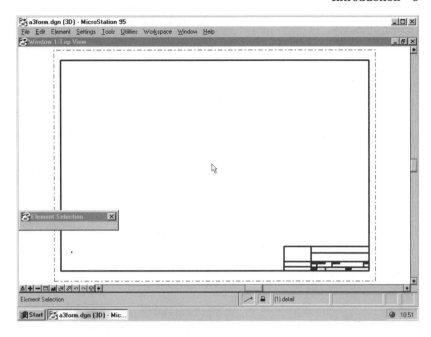

Fig. 1.9 Save the file to the filename **ay.dgn** in the **Save File As** dialogue box

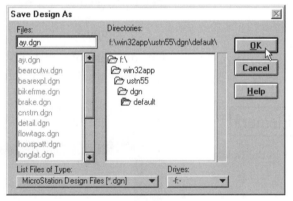

Fig. 1.10 *Left-click* on **Main** in the **Main** sub-menu of the **Tools** pull-down menu

2. In the **Tools** pull-down menu, select **Main**, **Standard** and **Primary** from the **Main** sub-menu (Fig. 1.10).

3. The **Main**, **Standard** and **Primary** toolboxes appear on screen (Fig. 1.11).

4. *Left-click* on the **Delete Element** tool icon in the **Main** tool palette (Fig. 1.12). With the tool delete all the borders and all of the title block, resulting in a screen as in Fig. 1.13.

5. *Left-click* on the **Start AccuDraw** icon in the **Primary** toolbox. The **AccuDraw** window appears on screen (Fig. 1.11).

6. *Drag* the tool boxes and the **AccuDraw** window to the side, top and bottom of the screen as shown in Fig. 1.13. The toolboxes lose their title bars and fit snugly against the edges of the MicroStation 95 window.

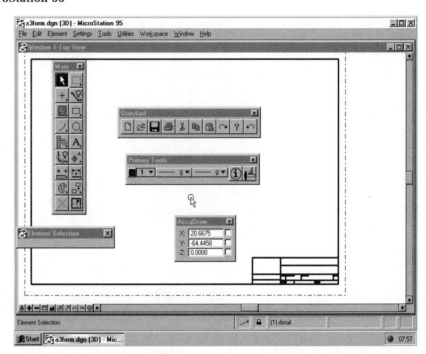

Fig. 1.11 The **Main**, **Standard** and **Primary** toolboxes appear on screen

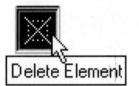

Fig. 1.12 Select the **Delete Element** tool

Stage 3

The default cursors for MicroStation 95 when the design file is opened is the Element Selection cursor. When a tool is active, the

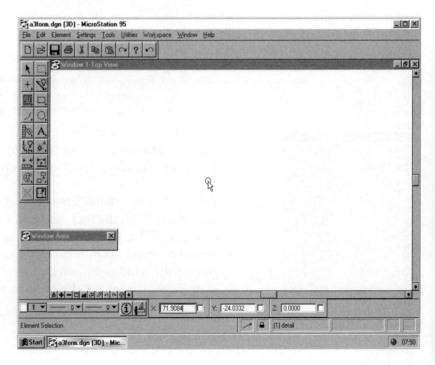

Fig. 1.13 Delete all parts of the borders and title block and *drag* toolboxes to positions as shown

Fig. 1.14 *Left-click* on
Preferences in the **Workspace**
pull-down menu

default cursor will change to one of two, either a small vertical cross
– **Normal** cursor (at the start of a tool operation) or a diagonal cross
(as the tool operation proceeds). A **Full View** cursor can be called to
screen if desired. Some operators may find this preferable to the
default cursors. To set **Full View** cursors:

1. *Left-click* on **Workspace** in the menu bar and in the pull-down
   menu which appears, *left-click* on **Preferences** (Fig. 1.14).
2. The **Preferences** dialogue box appears (Fig. 1.15).
3. *Left-click* on **Operations** in the dialogue box, followed by a *left-click* on **Full View** in the pop-up list against **Pointer Size** (Fig. 1.15).
   Then *left-click* on the **OK** button of the dialogue box. When a tool
   is selected, the cursor will be a pair of cross hairs, one vertical, the
   other horizontal, stretching the full height and width of the drawing
   area.

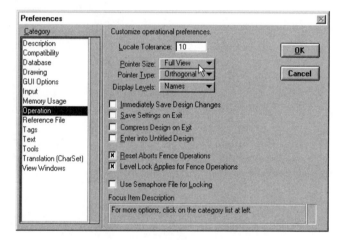

Fig. 1.15 *Left-click* on **Full
View** in the **Pointer Size** pop-
up list

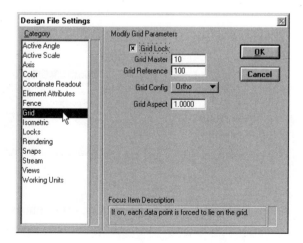

Fig. 1.16 Setting **Grid** in the
Design File Settings dialogue
box

Stage 4

1. *Left-click* on **Design File...** in the **Settings** pull-down menu and make settings in the **Design File Settings** dialogue box as in the following illustrations.

   (a) Set **Grid** in the **Design File Settings** dialogue box – Fig. 1.16.

   (b) Set the **Coordinate Readout** in the **Design Settings** dialogue box as shown in Fig. 1.17. Note once again, no figures after the decimal point.

   (c) Set **Snaps** as shown in Fig. 1.18.

   (d) Finally check that the **Working Units** are set in the **Design File Settings** dialogue box as shown in Fig. 1.19.

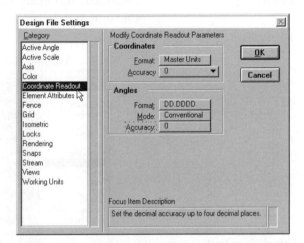

Fig. 1.17 Setting **Coordinate Readout** in the **Design File Settings** dialogue box

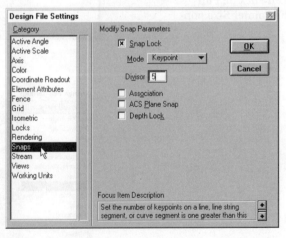

Fig. 1.18 Setting **Snaps** in the **Design File Settings** dialogue box

Stage 5

1. *Left-click* on **Preferences...** in the **Workspace** pull-down menu and in the **Preferences** dialogue box which then appears (Fig. 1.20); set

Fig. 1.19 Setting **Working Units** in the **design File Settings** dialogue box

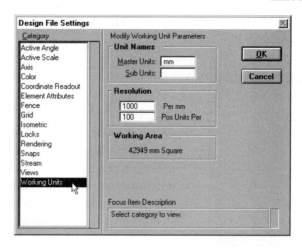

Fig. 1.20 Settings against **Operation** in the **Preferences** dialogue box

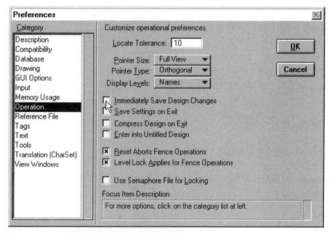

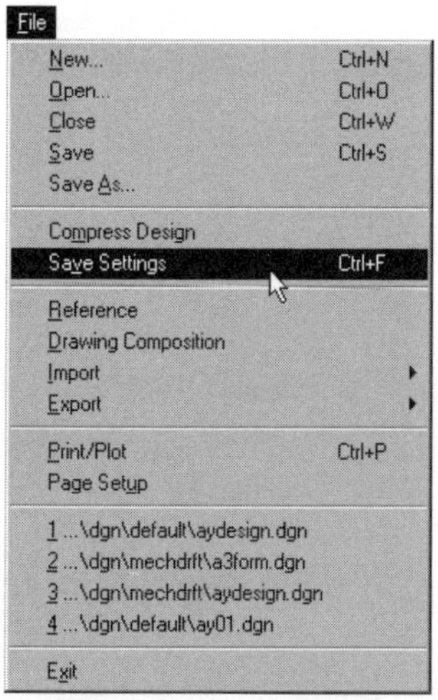

Operation as shown. Note in particular that the **Immediately Save Design Changes** and the **Save Settings on Exit** check boxes are set to off (no **X**) in the check boxes.

Stage 6

1. *Left-click* on **Save Settings** in the **File** pull-down menu (Fig. 1.21) to ensure that all the settings that have been made are saved with the design file.
2. In the **File** pull-down menu (Fig. 1.22) *left-click* on **Save As..** and save the file to dialogue box by *entering* the name **ay** in the **File:** box of the **Save Design As** dialogue box, followed by a *left-click* on the **OK** button of the dialogue box to save the file to disk with this name (Fig. 1.23).

Fig. 1.21 *Left-click* on **Save Settings** in the **File** pull-down menu

Fig. 1.22 *Left-click* on **Save As...** in the **File** pull-down menu

Fig. 1.23 In the **Save Design As** dialogue box *enter* the name **ay.dgn** in the file box

The resulting design file ay.dgn

Figure 1.24 shows the resulting design file screen for the **ay** file, showing the names of the principle parts of the screen.

A key-in window for the ay.dgn file

Select **Key-in** from the **Utilities** pull-down menu (Fig. 1.25). The **Key-in** dialogue box appears on screen (Fig. 1.26). Reduce the dialogue box to a key-in window as shown in Fig. 1.26. This window can be dragged into the bottom (or top) of the screen as shown in Fig. 1.27. This provides a **Key-in** field in the Status Bar for the **ay** prototype design file as shown in Fig. 1.27.

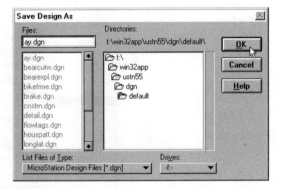

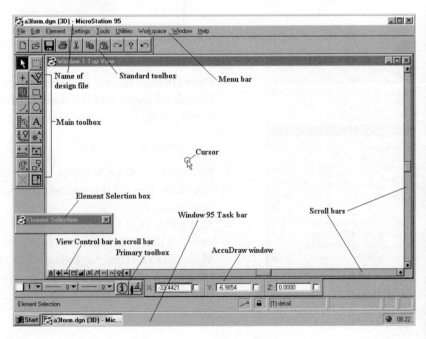

Fig. 1.24 The final design file **ay.dgn** with the principal parts named

Adding levels to the file

In the personal file described so far, only one level has been set – Level 1. That level has been set to use as the level on which outlines are to be drawn at a line weight of 1. Other levels can be set as follows.

Fig. 1.25 Select **Key-in** from the **Utilities** pull-down menu

Fig. 1.26 Stages in the fitting of a **Key-in** window in the Status Bar for the **ay.dgn** design file

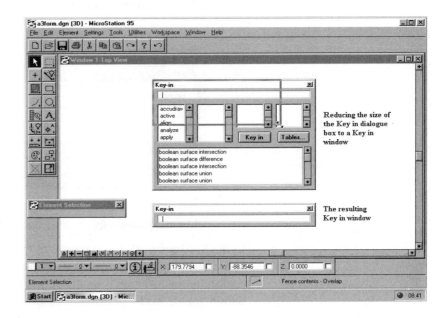

Fig. 1.27 The **ay.dgn** screen showing the names in the Status bar

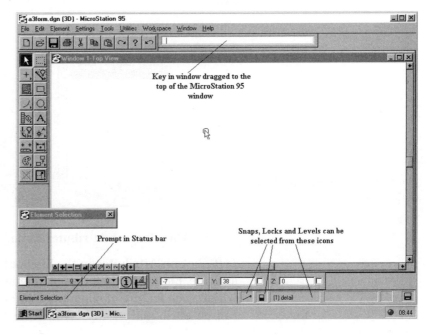

Level names

Left-click on **Level** in the **Settings** pull-down menu and again on **Names...** in the pull-down menu. The **Level Names** dialogue box appears (Fig. 1.28) in which names and details of names can be *entered* against the level numbers by using the **Add** button of the dialogue box. When all details have been added in the dialogue box *left-click* on the **Done** button.

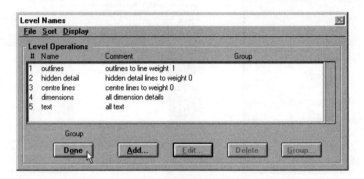

Fig. 1.28 The **Level Names** dialogue box

Level Symbology

In the **Settings** pull-down menu, *left-click* again on **Level** and in the sub-menu, *left-click* again on **Symbology**. The **Level Symbology** dialogue box appears (Fig. 1.29). In this dialogue box, colours, line weights and style of lines can be set against each of the level numbers.

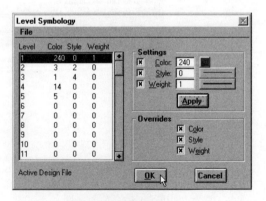

Fig. 1.29 The **Level Symbology** dialogue box

The Element Attributes dialogue box

Left-click on **Attributes** in the **Element** pull-down menu (Fig. 1.30) and the **Element Attributes** dialogue box appears (Fig. 1.31) in which each feature of elements – colour, line style and line weight can be attributed to any layer. Note the **Class** pop-up list which contains two classes – **Primary** and **Construction**. We are at the moment only concerned with the **Primary** class of element attributes.

Windows in MicroStation 95

Left-click on **Open/Close** in the **Windows** pull-down menu (Fig. 1.32) and a sub-menu appears showing that a choice may be made from 8 windows. *Left-click* on **2**, then on **3**, then on **4**, followed by another *left-click* on **Tile** in the **Windows** pull-down menu.

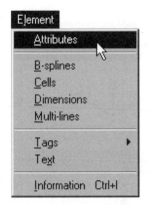

Fig. 1.30 Select Attributes from the **Element** dialogue box

Fig. 1.31 The **Element Attributes** dialogue box

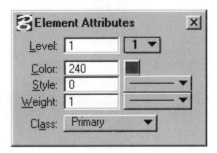

The ACS Triad

Select **View Attributes...** from the **Settings** pull-down menu and set the check box against **ACD Triad** in the resulting dialogue box on (**X** in check box) (Fig. 1.33). Then *left-click* on the **Apply** button. The **ACS Triad** appears in all four windows (Fig. 1.34)

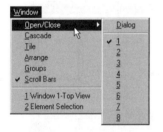

Fig. 1.32 Select windows for opening

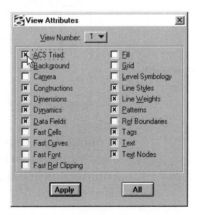

Fig. 1.33 Setting **ACS Triad** on in the **View Attributes** dialogue box

As many as eight windows

In all, eight windows can be brought to screen in MicroStation 95 as shown in Fig. 1.35. The operator therefore has the choice between

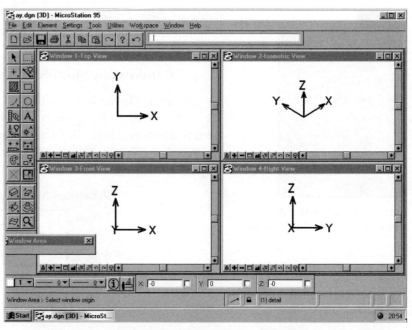

Fig. 1.34 The **ACS Triad** in four windows of a MicroStation screen

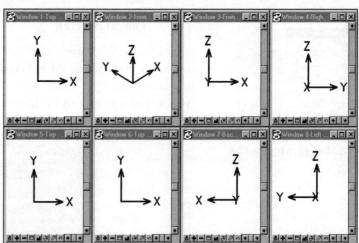

Fig. 1.35 The maximum eight-window screen with triad arrows showing

working in as many windows from a single window to as many as eight windows. In Fig. 1.35 all windows are showing the **ACS Triad**. Usually it is not necessary to have the triad arrows showing in any window.

The View Control bar

Unless the scroll bars in the windows are turned off the **View Control bar** shows in the lower scroll bar of each window. Figure 1.36 shows the bar with the names of the tool icons in the bar. The

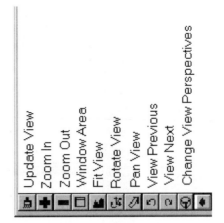

Fig. 1.36 The **View Control bar** with the names of the tools in the bar

operator is advised to make full use of the tools in these bars to manipulate the contents of the windows. In particular make full use of the **Fit View** tool, which fits whatever has been constructed within a window into the centre of the window. There may be times when the drawing in a window cannot be seen because it is outside the area covered by the window. A *left-click* on **Fit View** will bring the window contents into view.

If you do not wish to have scroll bars showing, *left-click* on **View Windows** in the **Preferences** dialogue box and set the **Scroll Bars on View Windows** check box off (no **X** in check box) as in Fig. 1.37. The result in a four-window screen will be as shown in Fig. 1.38.

Notes on the ACS Triad and the X,Y,Z axes

1. When working in 3D (three dimensions) there are three coordinates axes to contend with. These are the X, Y and Z axes. The **ACS Triad**

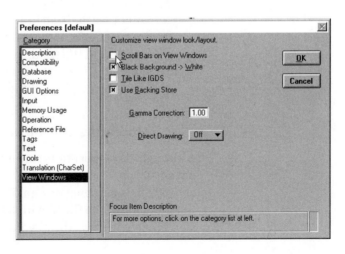

Fig. 1.37 Setting **Scroll Bars on View Windows** off

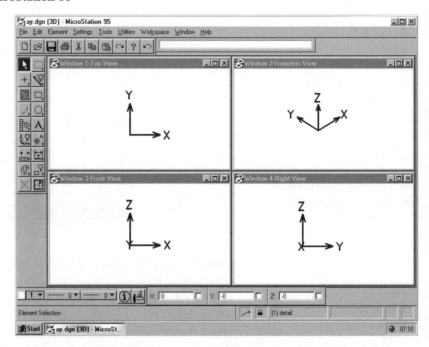

Fig. 1.38 A MicroStation screen with scroll bars turned off in all windows

shows clearly the directions of the axes in each view window, although common practice would be to work with the triads turned off.

2. If working mainly in the **Top View** window, it must be remembered that the Z axis is positive outwards from the screen towards the operator and the negative Z axis is away from the operator towards the computer.

3. When working in 3D in the other view windows, take careful note of the directions of all three axes as indicated in those illustrations showing the triads in this chapter.

4. The **ACS Triad** is at the coordinate X,Y,Z point which is 0,0,0. If you cannot see the triad in any window when it is turned on in **View Attributes**, use the **Pan** tool from the **View Control bar** to pan the window to find the triad.

5. In general, the X axis gives the width of a 3D model drawing, the Y axis gives the height and the Z axis gives the depth.

Operating note on saving the design screen

Although the **Operation** settings in the **Preferences** dialogue box have been set as shown in Fig. 1.20 on page 9, it is advisable, when calling one's personal design file to screen, to immediately save it to the filename of the file to which the drawing about to be constructed is to be saved. This allows your personal design file to be used over and over again without finding that the file has had elements added to it from the constructions from a previous drawing. Thus open the **File** pull-down menu by a *left-click* on **File** in the menu bar. Then select **Save As...** and when the **Save Design File** dialogue box appears, select a suitable directory and save the screen to the filename of the drawing about to be constructed.

Notes on Settings

1. It will have been noted in working through the details described in this chapter that some settings and preferences have been ignored. This is because the default settings of those that have not been deliberately set, have been accepted. However, the reader may wish to change these default settings for his/her own purposes.

2. All the illustrations in this book have been taken from a white background screen. This method has been adopted because it allows illustrations to be more easily followed. The reader may find it easier to work against a black background – some people find it more restful to the eyes than working against a white background. This setting can be made in **View Windows** option of the **Preferences** dialogue box.

3. All colours chosen for features in the given personal design file have been 0 or 240 (black on a white screen, white on a black screen) This again is because of the ease of showing black on white in a book illustration. The reader may well prefer working in other colours, perhaps with a different colour for each feature – say one for outline lines, another for hidden detail, another for centre lines, another for dimensions, another for text and so on.

4. A variety of colours for different levels may show up more clearly against a black screen than against a white screen. This will be seen in some of the colour plates.

Questions

1. What is the purpose of constructing your own personal design file?
2. Why do you think the borders were deleted from the **a3form.dgn** file when amending it to my **ay.dgn** file?
3. How is the **Key in** dialogue box called to screen?
4. How can a **Key in** window be placed in the Status Bar?
5. Do you know what the purpose is of having a **Key in** window on screen?
6. Can you understand why the **Working Units** are set as shown in Fig. 1.19 on page 9?

7. Do you know what the purpose is of the **AccuDraw Settings** dialogue box?
8. Why is it necessary to **Save Settings** when constructing a personal design file?
9. What is the purpose of the **ACS Triads**?
10. What is gained by turning the scroll bars in windows off? Why have them showing anyway?

CHAPTER 2

The Groups toolbox

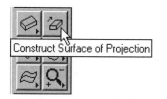

Fig. 2.1 Calling the **Construct Surface of Projection** tool

Fig. 2.2 Selecting **Phong Antialias** from the **Utilities** pull-down menu

Fig. 2.3 The two **Types** of surfaces of projection

Introduction

The tools in the **Groups** toolbox are important in the construction of the outlines from which some 3D models are constructed. Because of this we will discuss their use before going on to describing the construction of 3D model drawings in fuller detail.

In this chapter we will be using two tools which will be explained more fully in later chapters. These two tools are the **Construct Surface of Projection** tool from the **3D Tools** toolbox (Fig. 2.1) and **Phong Antialias** called from the **Utilities** pull-down menu (Fig. 2.2).

When the **Project Surface of Projection** tool is selected, the Element Selection box for the tool appears on screen. A *left-click* on the **Type** button brings down a pop-up list with two names – **Surface** and **Solid**. The two types are shown as selected from the **Type** button in Fig. 2.3.

Also for the purposes of showing the results of using the **Group** tools, a two-window screen will be shown – the **Window 1 – Top View** and **Window 2 – Isometric View**. In fact this is a fairly common set-up to use for the construction of 3D model drawing because much of the construction can be carried out in the **Top View** window, with the 3D results showing in the **Isometric View** window.

The Groups toolbox

In order to show the actions of the tools in the toolbox, the same outline constructed with the aid of the **Place Line** and **Place Circle**

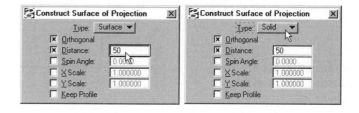

tools will be used for describing each of the tools. It must be noted here that if the **Smart Line** tool had been used to construct the outline, the use of the **Groups** tools would have been largely unnecessary. This is because the **Smart Line** tool produces a single element, which is itself in the form of a group. The **Place Line** tool forms a series of elements which, for our purposes here, must be formed into some type of group before the outline can be used as part of a 3D model.

Left-click on the **Drop Element** tool icon in the **Main** toolbox as shown in Fig. 2.4. The **Groups** flyout appears. *Drag* the flyout on screen and it changes to the **Groups** toolbox (Fig. 2.5). The names of the tools in the toolbox are shown in Fig. 2.5. *Taking each of the tools in turn.*

Fig. 2.4 Select the **Drop Element** from the **Main** toolbox

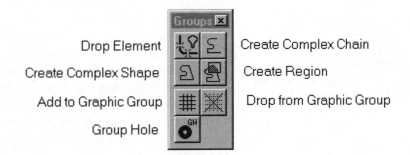

Fig. 2.5 The names of the tools in the **Groups** toolbox

The outline for demonstrating the Groups tools

With the aid of **Place Line** and **Place Circle**, followed by trimming parts of the circle with the aid of the **Trim Elements** tool, construct the outline shown in Fig. 2.6. Then with the **Construct Circular Fillet** tool add fillets of R10 as shown in Fig. 2.7. This gives us the outline we will be using in most of the illustrations in this chapter.

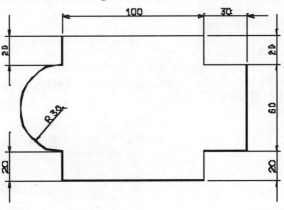

Fig. 2.6 The outline for demonstrating the use of the **Groups** tools

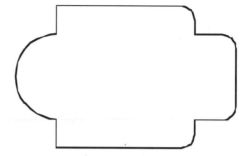

Fig. 2.7 The completed outline

The Create Complex Chain tool

Left-click on the **Create Complex Chain** tool in the **Groups** toolbox. The Status bar shows the prompt:

> **Create Complex Chain> Identify element** *left-click* on an element
> **Create Complex Chain> Accept/Reject (select next input)** *left-click* on the next element (see Fig. 2.8).

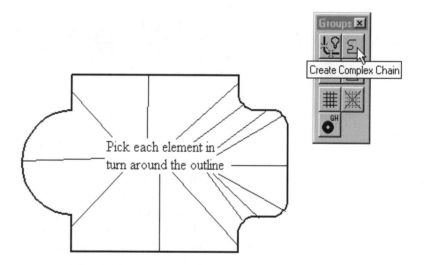

Fig. 2.8 Using the **Create Complex Chain** tool

Continue in this manner until all the elements in the outline have been *picked* in turn. When all have been *picked*, *right-click* and the group is formed. This can be checked by calling the **Move** tool and attempting to move the group. All the outline will move.

Now *left-click* on the **Construct Surface of Projection** tool. Its Element Selection box comes on screen. Set the check boxes against **Orthogonal** and **Distance** on (**X** in check box) *Enter* 50 in the **Distance** box, Followed by two *left-clicks* on the **Complex Chain** outline.

Then call **Phong Antialias** as shown in Fig. 2.2 and *left-click* in the **Isometric View** window. The surface of projection renders as shown in Fig. 2.9.

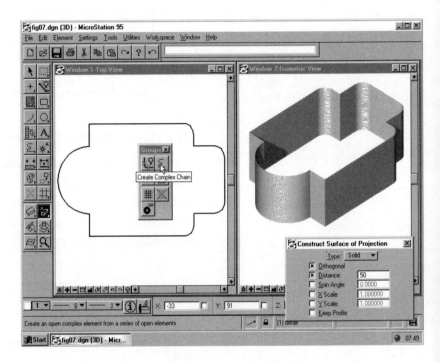

Fig. 2.9 The result of creating a surface of projection from a complex chain

Notes on the Create Complex Chain tool

1. It is important that the elements are *picked* in turn one after the other all around the outline. *Pick* one out of turn and the result will not be as desired. Try it.
2. It can be seen from Fig. 2.9, that a **Solid** cannot be created from a **Complex Chain**. The resulting projection in Fig. 2.9 is a surface – it has no top or bottom, only sides.
3. When using the **Construct Surface of Projection** tool, a surface of projection can be created from any single element as shown in Fig. 2.10. In Fig. 2.10, before using a **Groups** tool, three single elements were acted upon by the **Construct Surface of Projection** tool. Each of the elements forms a surface in its own right.

The Create Complex Shape tool

The method of using this tool is the same as for the **Create Complex Chain** tool, with the same prompts appearing at the Status bar as elements are *picked* in turn. However, when a surface of projection is created from the complex shape produced, a **Solid** of projection

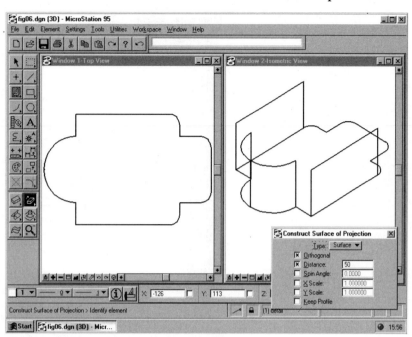

Fig. 2.10 Surfaces can be
created from single elements

can be created as shown in Fig. 2.11 – that is the projection has a top
and a bottom.

The procedure for creating the surface of projection illustrated in
Fig. 2.11 was:

1. Construct the outline with the **Place Line**, **Place Circle** and **Trim
   Elements** tools.
2. Call the **Create Complex Shape** tool and *pick* each element of the
   outline in turn. Two *left-clicks* completes the complex shape.
3. Call the **Construct Surface of Projection** tool. In its Element
   Selection box, set both the **Orthogonal** and **Distance** check boxes
   on.
4. *Enter* 50 in the **Distance** box.
5. *Left-click* on the complex shape. The surface of projection forms.
6. Call **Phong Antialias** and *left-click* in the **Isometric View** window.
7. The surface of projection renders.

The Group Hole tool

At the centre of the semicircle of the outline add an R15 circle. To
form a surface of projection from the complex shape and its circle:

1. Create a complex shape (not a complex chain) from the elements in
   the outline.
2. *Left-click* on the **Group Hole**. The prompts in the Status bar read:

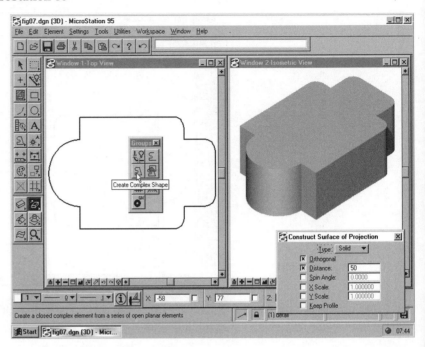

Fig. 2.11 A surface of projection formed from a complex shape

Group Holes> Identify Solid element *pick* the complex shape
Group Holes> Accept/Identify Hole element *pick* the circle *left-click*

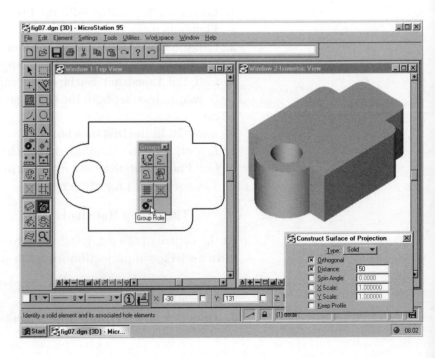

Fig. 2.12 A **Group Hole** in a solid of projection

3. *Left-click* on the **Construct Surface of Projection** tool.
4. Set **Orthogonal** on and **Distance** to 50 in the Element Selection box. Set **Type** to **Solid**.
5. *Pick* the complex shape and its hole. The surface of projection forms.
6. Call **Phong Antialias** and *left-click* in the **Isometric View** window. The result is shown in Fig. 2.12.

The Create Region tool

This tool will create groups from elements or from previously created complex chains or complex shapes. Figures 2.12 and 2.13 show stages in constructing a region outline from two blocks and a circle.

Stage 1: Draw the two blocks and the circle as shown in Fig. 2.13.

Stage 2: Figure 2.13. Select the **Create Region** tool and in its Element Selection box set the **Method** to **Difference** and make sure the check box for **Keep Original** is off (no **X** in check box). The Status bar options show:

Create Region from Element Difference> Identify element *left-click* on larger block.

Create Region from Element Difference> Accept/Reject (Identify next input) *left-click* on one of the smaller blocks.

Create Region from Element Difference> Identify additional/ Reset to complete *right-click.*

Repeat for the other smaller block.

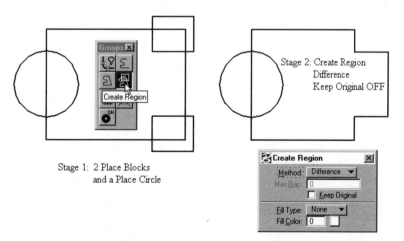

Stage 1: 2 Place Blocks
and a Place Circle

Fig. 2.13 Stages 1 and 2 in creating a region

Stage 3: Figure 2.14. Select the **Create Region** tool and in its Element Selection box set the **Method** to **Union** and make sure the check box

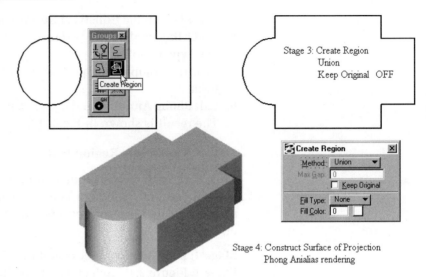

Fig. 2.14 Stages 3 and 4 in creating a region

Stage 3: Create Region
Union
Keep Original   OFF

Stage 4: Construct Surface of Projection
Phong Anialias rendering

for **Keep Original** is off (no **X** in check box). The Status bar options show:

Create Region from Element Difference> Identify element *left-click* on the created region.
Create Region from Element Difference> Accept/Reject (Identify next input) *left-click* on the circle.
Create Region from Element Difference> Identify additional/ Reset to complete *right-click*.

Stage 4: Figure 2.14. Create a surface of projection from the region and with **Phong Antialias** selected, render the 3D model.

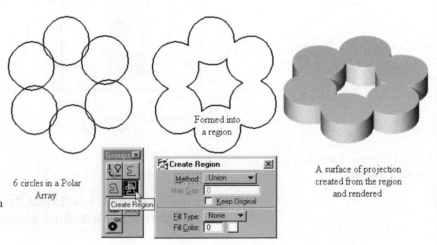

6 circles in a Polar Array

Formed into a region

A surface of projection created from the region and rendered

Fig. 2.15 A solid of projection formed from six interlocking circles

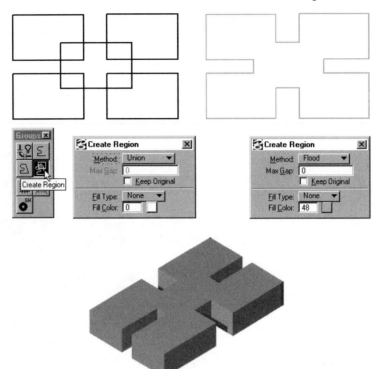

Fig. 2.16 Five intersecting blocks formed into a region and flood filled

Fig. 2.17 A rendering of the region from Fig. 2.16

Further examples of 3D models from groups

Figure 2.15 shows a Polar Array from six circles formed into a region with the **Create Region** tool and a surface of projection formed from the region, which is then rendered.

Figure 2.16 shows five intersecting blocks formed into a region with **Method** set to **Union**, followed by **Method** set to **Flood** and the

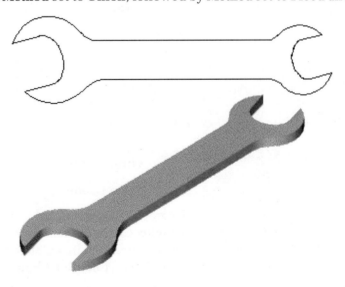

Fig. 2.18 The third example

Fig. 2.19 The fourth example

Fill Color set to 64 (a grey). Figure 2.17 shows the region formed into a surface of projection and rendered.

A third example is given in Fig. 2.18, in which the outline from the **Top View** window is shown together with a rendering of the surface of projection formed from the outline created from a complex shape.

A fourth example (Fig. 2.19) shows another spanner formed from a complex shape with group holes. The complex shape was then rendered as shown in the lower diagram of the two in the illustration.

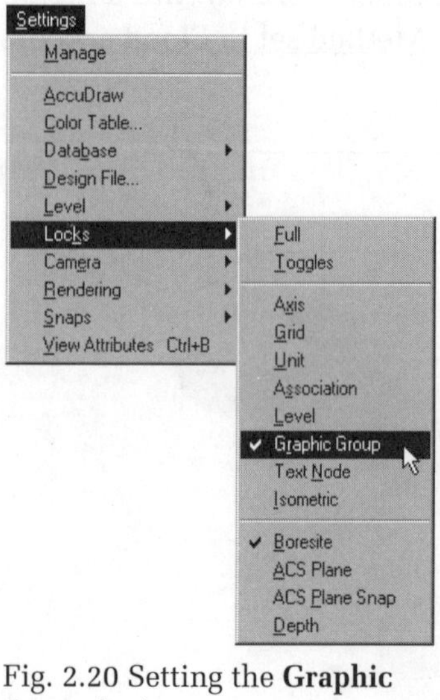

Graphic Group lock

In the **Settings** pull-down menu, *left-click* on **Locks**, followed by another on **Graphic Group** (Fig. 2.20). A tick then appears against the name **Graphic Group**, indicating that the lock for this item is on. When the lock is on, any action taken by a **Groups** tool acts upon the whole of the group. If off each element in a group is treated independently of the others in the group.

Other tools in the Groups toolbox

Open Groups

If a group is required that is not a closed area use either the **Create Complex Chain** or the **Add to Graphic Group** tools. An example is given in Fig. 2.21, in which the open group was formed with the aid of the **Create Complex Chain** tool.

Fig. 2.20 Setting the **Graphic Group** lock

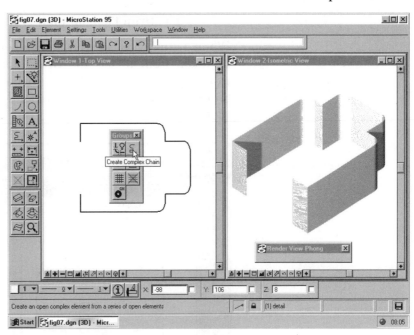

Fig. 2.21 An open group

The Add to Graphic Group tool

To add an element to an existing open group, use the **Add to Group** tool. Figure 2.22 shows a semicircle added to the group from that of Fig. 2.21.

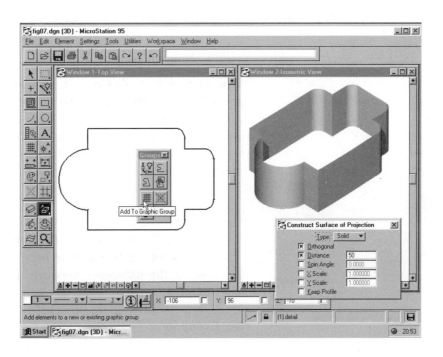

Fig. 2.22 Using the **Add to Graphic Group** tool

The Drop Element tool

When a group has been formed and elements from the group are to be taken from it, use the **Drop Element** tool. Figure 2.23 gives examples of elements which have been taken out (dropped) from a group and then moved away from the group with the aid of the **Move** tool.

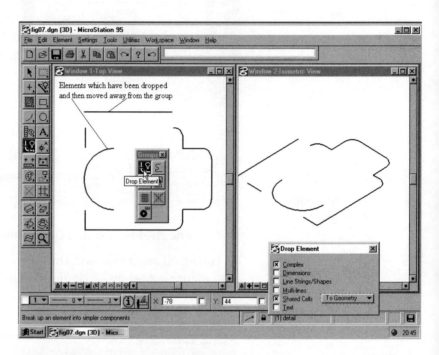

Fig. 2.23 Examples of the results of using **Drop Element**

Note on graphic groups

When using the tools **Create Complex Shape** or **Create Region**, the graphic group which is formed can be rendered without necessarily forming a surface of projection from the group. A surface is formed when a set of elements is formed into a group from the use of these tools. This has important uses when it is necessary to construct a plane surface.

Questions

1. Why are the tools in the **Groups** toolbox so important when constructing 3D model drawings?
2. What is the difference between the results of using the **Create Complex Chain** tool and using the **Create Complex Shape** tool?
3. Can a complex chain be constructed with the **Add to Graphic Group** tool?

4. Have you tried using the **Create Region** tool with **Union** set in the **Method** box?
5. What is the purpose of the **Drop Element** tool?
6. Can the **Create Region** tool be used in place of the **Group Hole** tool in some circumstances?
7. How can a plane surface be generated from using the tools in the **Groups** toolbox?
8. What are the differences resulting from the **Create Region** and the **Graphic Hole** tools?
9. Can you describe the differences in the results of setting the **method** when using **Create Region** between **Union, Intersection** and **Difference**?
10. What happens when using the **Create Graphic Shape** tool when an element is *picked* out of turn?

Exercises

1. The left-hand drawing of Fig. 2.24 shows the outline of the group from which the rendering to the right-hand of the drawing was created. The procedure was:
    (a) construct the given outline.
    (b) form a graphic group from the elements in the outline.
    (c) with **Move Parallel** create a second outline inside the first at 5 units distance.
    (d) with **Create Region** (with **Method** set to **Difference**) create a region.
    (e) create a surface of projection from the region.

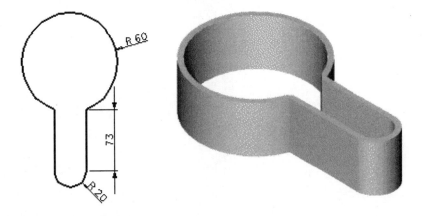

Fig. 2.24 Exercise 1

2. The left-hand drawing of Fig. 2.25 shows dimensioned views of the three parts making up the rendered 3D model shown in the right-

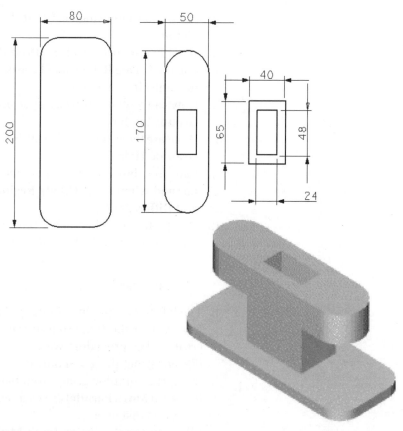

Fig. 2.25 Exercise 2

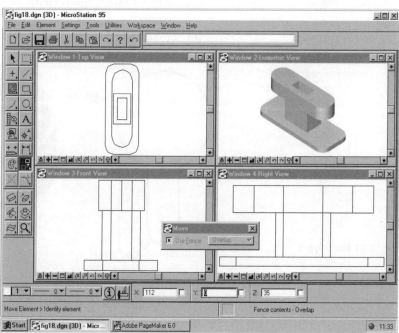

Fig. 2.26 Exercise 2. Note the movement of the three parts in the **Front View** window

hand part of the illustration. The base is 10 high, the central part is 50 high and the top part 30 high.

Figure 2.26 shows how the three parts were adjusted into position in the **Front View** window with the aid of the **Move** tool.

It must be noted that unless the **ACS** (Auxiliary Coordinate System) **Plane** lock is off as set in the **Locks** sub-menu of the **Settings** pull-down menu, you will find you will be unable to move the parts of the model in the **Front View** window in a vertical position. This is because the **ACS** plane is at the base of the **Front View** window. Unlocking the **ACS** plane allows movement vertically in that window.

More about the **ACS** plane and using **Move** to move surfaces of projection will be given in later chapters. For the time being work this exercise as suggested, without bothering too much about the implications of the **ACS** plane.

3. The upper drawing of Fig. 2.27 shows the dimensions for the group from which the rendering of the 3D model shown in the lower part of the illustration was formed. The model is 10 units high.

    Construct the outline and form it into a group, which can be acted upon by the **Construct Surface of Projection** tool.

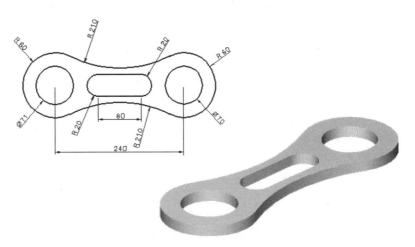

Fig. 2.27 Exercise 3

4. Figure 2.28 is a dimensioned drawing of a group from which the rendered 3D model shown in Fig. 2.29 was obtained.

    Construct the group using the most suitable **Groups** tool.

5. Figure 2.30 shows a dimensioned top view and an isometric view of a surface of projection. Construct the 3D model shown using the most suitable tools.

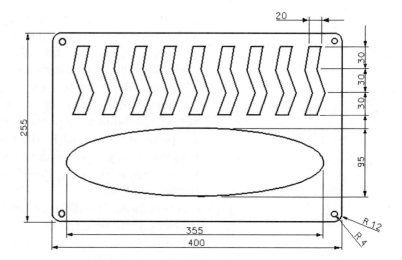

Fig. 2.28 Exercise 4

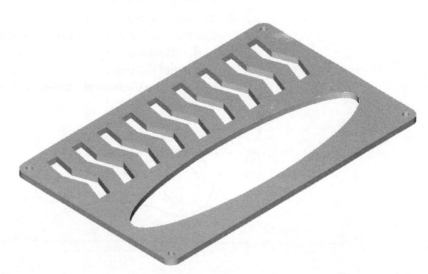

Fig. 2.29 A rendering of
Exercise 4

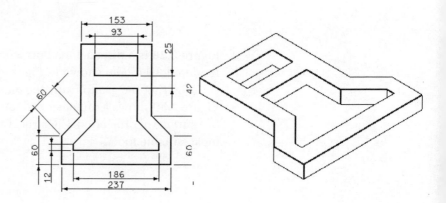

Fig. 2.30 Exercise 5

CHAPTER 3

The 3D Free-form Surfaces toolbox

Introduction

In this chapter we deal with the variety of surfaces and solids which can be constructed with tools from the **3D Free-form Surfaces** toolbox.

Before going on to this description, first ensure that the **3D Tools** toolbox is brought onto screen and *dragged* to the left-hand side of the MicroStation 95 window. To call the toolbox, *left-click* on **3D** in the **Tools** pull-down menu (Fig. 3.1) and *drag* the resulting **3D Tools** toolbox to the left-hand side of the MicroStation 95 window just under the **Main** toolbox (Fig. 3.2).

Fig. 3.1 Calling the **3D Tools** toolbox to screen

The 3D Free-form Surfaces toolbox

Hold down the left-hand button of the mouse over the **Construct Surface of Projection** tool icon in the **3D Tools** toolbox and the **3D Free-form Surfaces** flyout appear (Fig. 3.3).

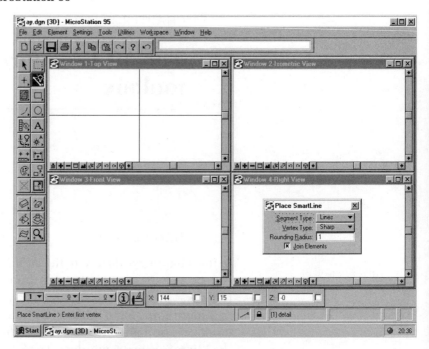

Fig. 3.2 The **3D Tools** toolbox
fitted under the **Main** toolbox

Fig. 3.3 The **3D Free-form
Surfaces** flyout

Drag the flyout away from the toolbox and the **3D Free-form
Surfaces** toolbox appears (Fig. 3.4). Figure 3.4 includes the names of
all the tools in the toolbox.

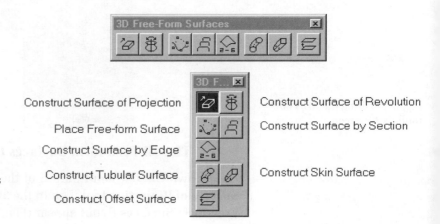

Fig. 3.4 The names of the tools
in the **3D Free-form Surfaces**
toolbox

Construct Surface of Projection

Fig. 3.5 The **Construct Surface of Projection** tool

The Construct Surface of Projection tool

This tool has already been partly described in Chapter 2, together with some of the possible solids resulting from its use. Further examples are given below. It will be remembered that either surfaces or solids can be constructed with the aid of this tool – refer back to Chapter 2.

Use of the Construct Surface of Projection tool

In the following examples the outline Fig. 3.6 will be used as the basis from which the solids and surfaces are created. It is a group.

The examples shown below have been rendered with the **Filled Hidden Line** tool from the **Utilities** pull-down menu (Fig. 3.7).

Fig. 3.6 The outline from which surfaces of projection will be created

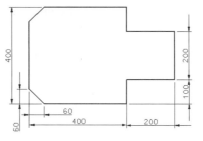

Fig. 3.7 Calling the **Filled Hidden Line** tool

First example (Fig. 3.8)

Select the **Construct Surface of Projection tool** and in its Element Selection box, set the **Type:** to **Solid**. Set the check boxes against **Orthogonal:** and **Distance:** on (**X** in check boxes). *Enter* 100 in the **Distance:** box and *left-click* on the outline. Figure 3.7 shows the resulting solid model rendered with the **Filled Hidden Line** tool.

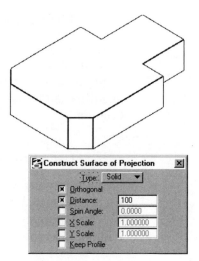

Fig. 3.8 First example

Second example (Fig. 3.9)

Change the **Type:** to **Surface** and *Enter* 150 in the **Distance:** box, followed by a *left-click* on the outline in the **Isometric View** window and the result is as shown in Fig. 3.9.

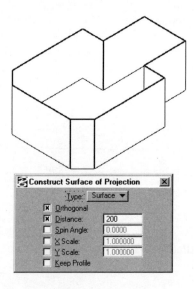

Fig. 3.9 Second example

Third example (Fig. 3.10)

With **Type:** set to **Solid** and with all check boxes in the Element Selection box off (no **X**s in the check boxes) *drag* the outline vertically with the aid of the **AccuDraw** compass. *Enter* 300 in the **X** window of the **AccuDraw** window. Then *left-click* on the outline in the **Isometric View** window. Then call the **Filled Hidden Line** tool and *left-click* in the **Isometric** window. The result will be as shown in Fig. 3.10.

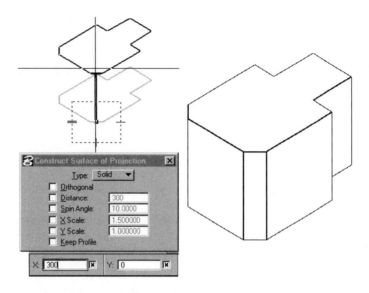

Fig. 3.10 Third example

Fourth example (Fig. 3.11)

With **Type:** set to **Solid** in the Element Selection box and with the check boxes against **Distance:** and **Spin Angle:** set on, *enter* 150 in the **Distance:** box and 10 in the **Spin Angle:** box. Then *left-click* on the outline in the **Isometric View** window, followed by rendering with **Filled Hidden Line**. The results will be as shown in Fig. 3.11.

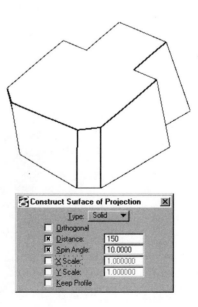

Fig. 3.11 Fourth example

Fig. 3.12 The **Construct Surface of Revolution** tool icon

Use of the Construct Surface of Revolution tool

The first two examples of the use of this tool are surfaces of revolution derived from the outline Fig. 3.13. After constructing the outline with the **Place Circle**, **Place Line** and **Trim** tools, the outline was formed into a group with the aid of the **Create Complex Chain** tool.

Fig. 3.13 The outline from which the first two examples of surfaces of revolution were created

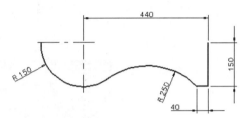

First example (Fig. 3.14)

Call the tool (Fig. 3.12) and in its Element Selection box, set the **Type:** to **Solid**, the **Axis:** to **Points (AccuDraw)** and *enter* 360 in the **Angle:** box. The **Keep Profile** check box should be off (no **X** in the check box).

In the **Isometric View** window, *left-click* on the outline and *double-click* (i.e. a tentative point) on one end of the profile to set its snap point, followed by a *left-click* on the snap point, then repeat at the other end of the outline. The surface of revolution forms.

Call **Phong Antialias** from the **Utilities** pull-down menu and *left-click* in the **Isometric View** window. The surface of revolution renders as shown in Fig. 3.14.

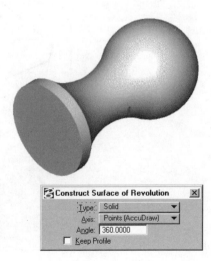

Fig. 3.14 First example

Second example (Fig. 3.15)

Call the tool, and in its Element Selection box, set the **Type:** to **Surface**, the **Axis:** to **Points (AccuDraw)** and the **Angle:** to 90. In the **Isometric View** window, *left-click* on the outline, followed by tentative points at each end of the outline (*double-clicks*, followed by a *left-click* each end), followed by a *right-click*. Note that it must be a *right-click*. If a *left-click* is given when the surface of revolution forms, a second 90° surface will form and a third after another (wrong) *left-click*. Now render with **Filled Hidden Line**. The result will be as in Fig. 3.15.

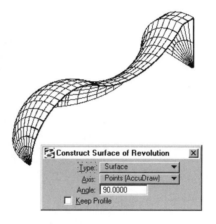

Fig. 3.15 Second example

Third example (Fig. 3.17)

The following four examples are based on the outline constructed in the **Top View** window (Fig. 3.16). After constructing the outline, form it into a group with the aid of the **Create Complex Shape** tool.

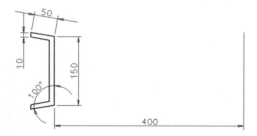

Fig. 3.16 The outline from which Examples 3 to 6 have been created

Call the **Construct Surface of Revolution** tool and in its Element Selection box, set **Type:** to **Solid**, **Axis:** to **Points (AccuDraw)** and *enter* 360 in the **Angle:** box.

Then in the **Isometric View** window, *left-click* on the outline followed by *double-clicks* and *left-clicks* at each end of the line drawn at 400 units from the outline. The surface of revolution forms. Render with **Phong Antialias** with the result as shown in Fig. 3.17.

Fig. 3.17 Third example

Fourth example (Fig. 3.18)

Follow the same procedure as for the first example, except that the **Angle:** setting is *entered* as 90°. Again beware of *left-clicks* after the surface forms at 90°. A *left-click* at this stage will form a 180° surface, a further *left-click* will form a 270° surface and a third a 360° surface.

When the quadrant has formed render with **Phong Antialias**. The result is shown in Fig. 3.18.

Fig. 3.18 Fourth example

Fifth example (Fig. 3.19)

For this example make the following settings in the tool's Element Selection box – **Type: Surface**, **Axis: Screen X**, **Angle:** 360.

Then with the aid of the **Midpoint** snap, *left-click* at the centre of the right-hand edge of the outline to determine the **X** point. Then *left-click* again. The surface of revolution forms. Render with **Filled Hidden Line**. The result is as shown in Fig. 3.19.

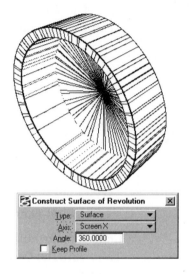

Fig. 3.19 Fifth example

Sixth example (Fig. 3.20)

For this example make the following settings in the tool's Element Selection box – **Type: Surface**, **Axis: Screen Y**, **Angle:** 360.

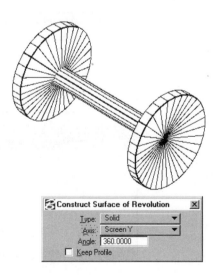

Fig. 3.20 Sixth example

Then with the aid of the **Midpoint** snap, *left-click* at the centre of the right-hand edge of the outline to determine the **Y** point. Then *left-click* again. The surface of revolution forms. Render with **Filled Hidden Line**. The result is as shown in Fig. 3.20.

Fig. 3.21 The **Construct Surface by Section** tool

Use of the Construct Surface by Section tool

The first two examples were created from the outline given in Fig. 3.22. The outline was drawn with the aid of **Place Line**, **Place Circle**, **Trim Element** and **Create Complex Chain**.

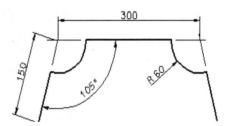

Fig. 3.22 The outline for the first two examples

First example (Fig. 3.24)

Construct the outline shown in Fig. 3.22 in the **Front View** window. Then with the **Copy** tool copy the group in the **Right View** window four times with a spacing of 50 between each copy as shown in Fig. 3.23. If necessary *left-click* on the **Fit View** tool icon in the scroll bars to fit the resulting views in their respective windows.

Left-click on the **Construct Surface by Section** tool icon. Prompts in the Status bar show:

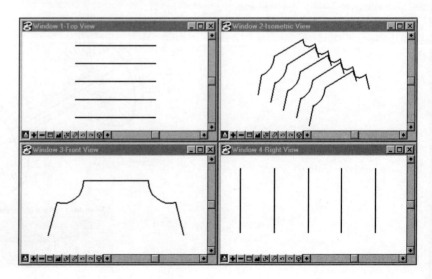

Fig. 3.23 Constructing the section curves for the first example

Surface by Section or Network>Identify first section curve

Ensure that the **Define by:** box is set for **Section**, then *left-click* on each section curve in turn, followed by a *left-click* after selecting all the curves. This results in the surface being formed. Figure 3.24 shows the surface formed by this procedure after the resulting surface has been rendered with the aid of **Phong Antialias**.

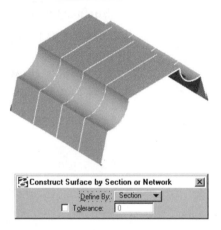

Fig. 3.24 First example

Second example (Fig. 3.26)

This example shows a surface formed by the use of the **Construct Surface by Section** tool from a network. The network must have both **V** lines – the surface curves as seen from the front and **U** lines connecting the **V** lines. In this second example, the same surface curves were used, but they were connected together with lines added with the aid of the **AccuDraw** compass and suitable tentative snap points. The resulting network of V and U lines is shown in Fig. 3.25.

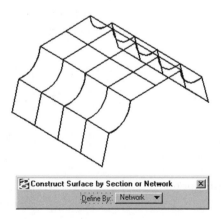

Fig. 3.25 The network for the second example

Select the **Construct Surface by Section** tool and in its Element Selection box set **Network** in the **Define by:** box. The Status bar prompts display:

Surface by Section or Network>Identify first U section curve

Select each U section curve in turn, then *left-click*. The Status bar then shows:

Surface by Section or Network>Identify first V section curve

Select each V line (or curve) in turn, followed by a *left-click*. The surface forms.

Figure 3.26 shows the second example after the surface has been formed and after rendering with **Phong Antialias**.

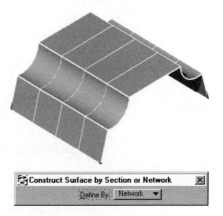

Fig. 3.26 Second example

Third example (Fig. 3.28)

The surface curve for this example is given in Fig. 3.27. Construct the outline for the surface curve in the **Front View** window and make a second copy of the outline in the **Right view** window at a distance of 100 from the first. Then select the **Construct Surface by Section** tool, set **Define by:** to **Section** and *left-click* on both surface curves one after the other, followed by another *left-click*. The surface forms.

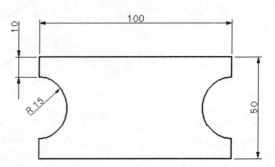

Fig. 3.27 The outline for the third example

Figure 3.28 shows the results after rendering with **Filled Hidden Line**.

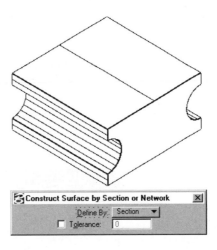

Fig. 3.28 Third example

Use of the Construct Surface by Edges tool

The **Construct Surface from Edges** tool (Fig. 3.29) can be used to form surfaces from between two and six lines, arcs or curves in 3D space. Except when forming a surface from two lines, arcs or curves, the outline formed from the curves must be a closed loop. If an attempt is made to form a surface from a set of curves and there is even the smallest gap between the ends of any two adjacent curves, a message appears at the Status bar:

Error: Curves do not form a closed loop

First example – from two curves (Fig. 3.32)

Fig. 3.29 The **Construct Surface by Edges** tool icon

Construct the two curves as shown in Fig. 3.29. The front curve was constructed from four arcs which were formed into a group with the aid of the **Construct Graphic Chain** tool. The group was then copied in the **Right View** window as shown to form the two curves for this example (Fig. 3.30).

Call the **Construct Surface by Edges** tool. The Status bar shows the prompt:

Construct Surface by Edges > Identify first edge *pick* one of the curves.
Construct Surface by Edges > Identify next edge or miss *pick* the second curve.
Construct Surface by Edges > Identify next edge or miss *left-click.*

Construct Surface by Edges > Accept/Reject *left-click.*

and the surface forms in a ghosted form. *Left-click* to accept the surface and the ghosted forms changes to the original colours of the curves (Fig. 3.31).

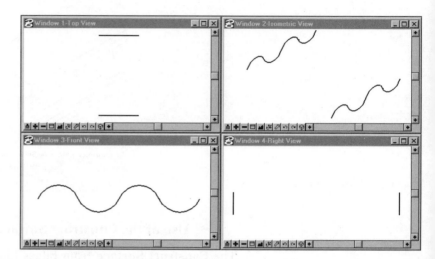

Fig. 3.30 The four-window screen when constructing the curves for the first example

Figure 3.32 shows the surface after being rendered with the aid of the **Phong Antialias** tool.

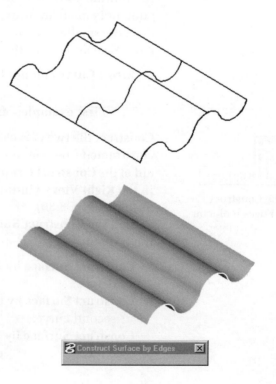

Fig. 3.31 The surface of the first example

Fig. 3.32 First example

Second example – from five curves (Fig. 3.34)

No matter how many curves from which the surface is to be formed – from two to a maximum of six, the procedures for creating the surface with this tool are the same. However, the loop formed by the curves must be closed and the curves in the loop must be *picked* in turn one after the other.

Figure 3.33 shows the loop as seen in the **Isometric View** window, from which the surface for second example was formed and Fig. 3.34 the surface after being formed and then rendered with the aid of **Phong Antialias**.

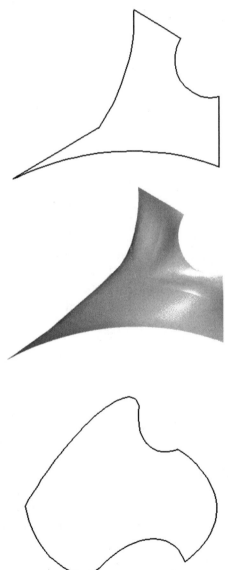

Fig. 3.33 The outline loop from five curves for the second example

Fig. 3.34 The second example after being rendered

Fig. 3.35 The loop formed from six curves for the third example

Third example – from six curves (Fig. 3.36)

Figure 3.35 shows the loop formed by six curves in the **Isometric View** window for the third example and Fig. 3.36 the loop after being rendered with **Phong Antialias**.

Fig. 3.36 The third example after rendering

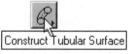

Fig. 3.37 Selecting the **Construct Tubular Surface** tool

Use of the Construct Tubular Surface tool

When this tool is called (Fig. 3.27) its Element Selection box allows two types of tubular surface to be created – **Solid** and **Surface**. If the tubular surface is to be defined by a circular section, then the inside and outside radii of the tubular section can be set in the respective radius boxes. If a section curve other than circular is required the outline of the section must be included with the trace curve of the tube. Figures 3.38 and 3.39 show the Element Selection box for the tool with the choices in the pop-up lists.

Fig. 3.38 The pop-up list for **Type:**

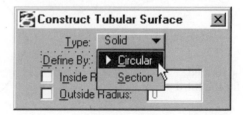

Fig. 3.39 The pop-up list for **Define by:**

First example (Fig. 3.40)

This example shows the result of first drawing a line, followed by calling the tool and making settings as shown in Fig. 3.40 in the Element Selection box. When the tool is called the Status bar prompt is:

Construct tubular surface > Identify trace curve *pick* the line.
Construct tubular surface > Accept/Reject *left-click* (twice).

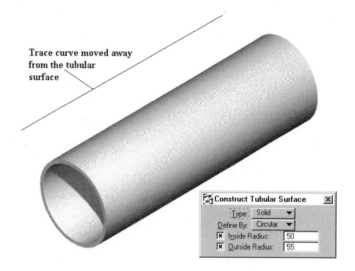

Fig. 3.40 First example

Second example (Fig. 3.41)

The trace curve for this example was constructed with the aid of the **Smart Line** tool with the **Vertex Type:** set to **Chamfered** in the Element Selection box. After making settings in the tool's selection box as shown in Fig. 3.41, the tubular surface was formed in exactly the same way as in the previous example.

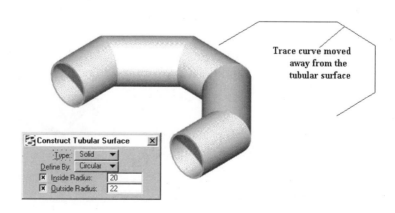

Fig. 3.41 Second example

Third example (Fig. 3.42)

The trace curve for this example was constructed from two touching circles, which were trimmed to produce two touching 270° circles, which were then formed into a group with the **Construct Complex Chain** tool. Then the construction of the tubular surface followed the procedures as for the two previous examples.

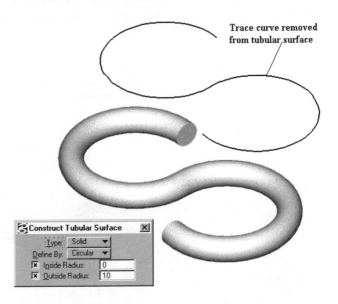

Fig. 3.42 Third example

Fourth example (Fig. 3.43)

As can be seen from Fig. 3.43 the settings in the tool's Element Selection box was for a tubular surface created from a section – in this case a hexagon. The hexagon was drawn at the end of the trace curve in the **Right View** window. The prompts in the Status bar for this example were:

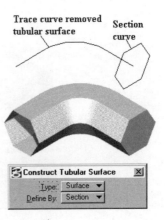

Fig. 3.43 Fourth example

Construct Tubular Surface > Identify trace curve *pick.*
Construct Tubular Surface > Identify and Accept/Reject section curve *pick* section curve (the hexagon) then *left-click.*

Note that the section curve renders, even though this is of a **Type:** surface – the section curve is treated as if it were a surface.

Notes

1. The trace curve is not erased automatically when a tubular surface is formed, but can be erased independently of the surface.
2. In all the examples of tubular surface given above, the trace curves have been moved away from the rendered surfaces. This method of showing the trace curves has been adopted here merely for illustrative purposes.
3. When constructing tubular surfaces if a rounded corner (or fillet) is smaller in radius than the section curve, the tubular surface will be distorted.
4. In general tubular surfaces can only be constructed from trace curves lying in a single plane.

Exercises

1. The rendering of a 3D model shown in Fig. 3.44 has been created from the outline shown in the left-hand drawing of Fig. 3.44. Copy the given outline and from it construct the 3D model

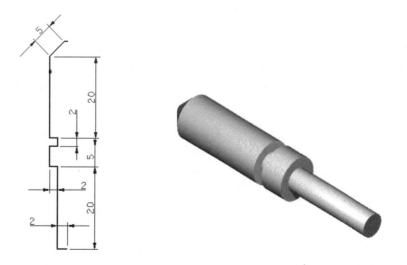

Fig. 3.44 Exercise 1

Fig. 3.45 Exercise 2

2. Figure 3.45 shows a rendering of an Allen key. Working to any suitable sizes, construct a 3D model of an Allen key similar to that shown in Fig. 3.45.
3. Figures 3.46 and 3.47 given details of a handle to be attached to a hand machine tool. Working to the dimensions given in Fig. 3.46, construct the 3D model shown rendered in Fig. 3.47.

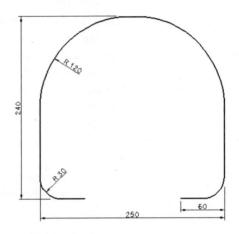

Fig. 3.46 Outline for Exercise 3

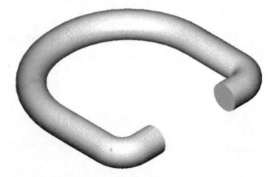

Fig. 3.47 the rendering of Exercise 3

4. Figure 3.48 shows the dimensions of the outlines from which the adjust lever given in the 3D model of Fig. 3.49 was constructed. Construct the 3D model from the given information in the two illustrations.

Fig. 3.48 Dimensioned drawing for Exercise 4

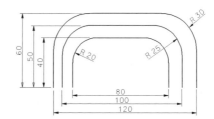

Fig. 3.49 A rendering of the model for Exercise 4

5. Figure 3.50 gives the dimensions of the section curves from which the 3D model of Fig. 3.51 was constructed. Construct the 3D model to the given information.

Fig. 3.50 Dimensioned drawing of the section curves for Exercise 5

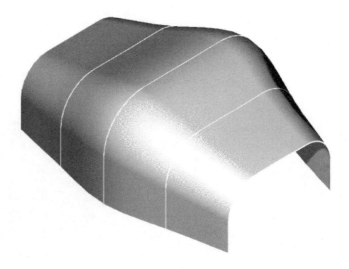

Fig. 3.51 Exercise 5

6. The three illustrations Figs 3.52–3.54 show the details from which the answer to this exercise can be constructed. Construct the 3D model shown rendered in Fig. 3.54.

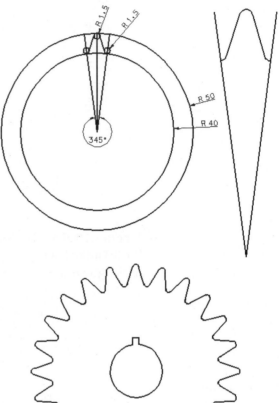

Fig. 3.52 Dimensions for Exercise 6

Fig. 3.53 The outline from which the 3D model for Exercise 3 was created

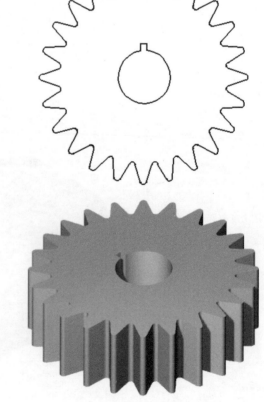

Fig. 3.54 Exercise 6

CHAPTER 4

More 3D Free-form Surfaces tools

Introduction

Examples of the use of three tools from the **3D Free-form Surfaces** toolbox not described in Chapter 3 will be given in this chapter. These three tools are the **Place Free-form Surface** tool, the **Construct Skin Surface** tool and the **Construct Offset Surface** tool.

The Place Free-form Surface tool

Fig. 4.1 The **Place Free-form Surface** tool icon

Select the tool (Fig. 4.1) and the tool's Element Selection box appears. In the Element Selection box:

Method: can be chosen, of which two examples are given – **Through Points** and **Define Poles**.

Define by: can be chosen – of which **Placement** is shown here.

Closure: the surface can be **Open** or **Closed**. Both the examples here will be open.

Order of U and V lines can be *entered*. The first example will be four V and four U lines.

First example (Fig. 4.3)

Call the tool. Set **Method:** to **Through Points**. Set **Define by:** to **Placement**. Set **Closure:** to **Open**. **Order:** U *enter* 4; V *enter* 4. The Status bar prompts show:

Place Free-form Surface > Enter start point in the **Top View** window; *left-click* at point **1** (Fig. 4.2).

Place Free-form Surface > Enter next point, or RESET to finish row *left-click* at point **2**.

Place Free-form Surface > Enter next point, or RESET to finish row *left-click* at point **3**.

Place Free-form Surface > Enter next point, or RESET to finish row *left-click* at point **4** followed by a *right-click*.

Place Free-form Surface > Enter next point, or RESET to finish row *left-click* at point **5**.

Now continue in this manner until point **16** is reached (Fig. 4.2). Then *right-click*. The surface forms (Fig. 4.3).

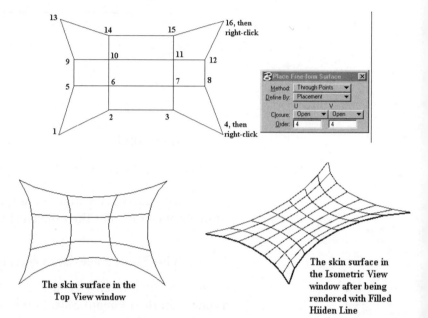

Fig. 4.2 Order of *entering* points for the free-form surface

Fig. 4.3 First example

The skin surface in the Top View window

The skin surface in the Isometric View window after being rendered with Filled Hidden Line

Notes

1. Only two *right-click* (RESETs) are used – at the end of the first row and at the end of the whole sequence.
2. The resulting surface is formed from B-spline curves.

Second example (Fig. 4.4)

In this example the settings in the tool's Element Selection box were:

Method: Define Poles.
Define by: Placement.
Closure: Open.
Order: U 3; V 3.

The poles were *picked* by working in two view windows – **Top View** and **Front View**, alternating between them and watching the **Isometric View** window to check on the results. Figure 4.4 shows the four windows when all points had been *picked*, thus completing the surface. The surface in the **Isometric View** window has been rendered with the aid of **Phong Antialias**.

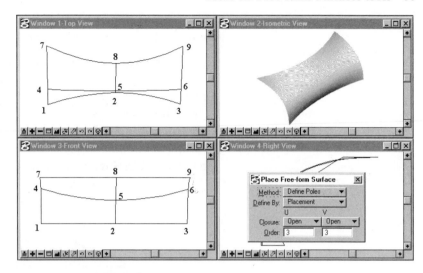

Fig. 4.4 Second example

The Construct Skin Surface tool

Fig. 4.5 The **Construct Skin Surface** tool icon

This tool can be used to form surfaces from two grouped outlines (section curves) connected by a single line or curve (the trace curve).

First example (Fig. 4.7)

Construct the two section curves – in this example they are arcs. Construct the trace curve – note it need not be in contact with either of the two section curves although in this example the trace curve connects the two section curves. The trace curve can however be independent of the two section curves. But take care – it must be in line with the section curves.

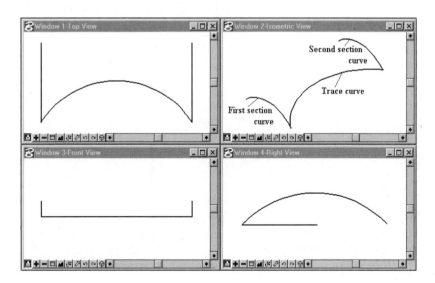

Fig. 4.6 The four windows showing the trace curve and section curves for the first example

Call the tool (Fig. 4.5). In the tool's Element Selection box set **Type:** to **Surface**. The Status bar prompts show:

Construct Skin Surface > Identify trace curve *pick* the trace curve.

Construct Skin Surface > Identify first section curve *pick* either section curve.

Construct Skin Surface > Identify second section curve *pick* the other section curve.

Construct Skin Surface > Accept/Reject *left-click* to accept. The surface forms (Fig. 4.7).

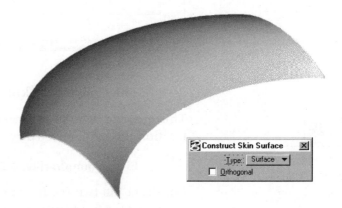

Fig. 4.7 First example

Second example (Fig. 4.9)

In this example, the section curves are grouped lines and arcs. Call the tool and *pick* the trace curve and section curves in turn (Fig. 4.8) and the surface forms. Figure 4.9 shows the surface after rendering with the aid of **Phong Antialias**.

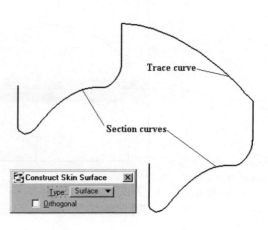

Fig. 4.8 Trace curve and section curves for second and third examples

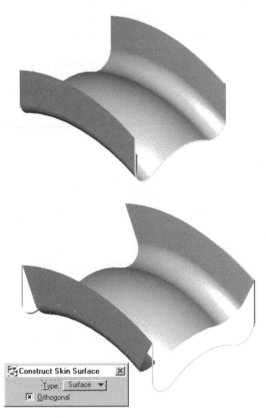

Fig. 4.9 Second example

Fig. 4.10 Third example

Third example (Fig. 4.10)

This example uses the same trace curve and section curves as were used for the second example. However, in the tool's Element Selection box, the check box against **Orthogonal** was set on (**X** in check box).

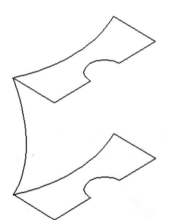

Fig. 4.11 The trace and section curves for the fourth example

Fig. 4.12 Fourth example

When the surface forms it is orthogonal (at right angles) to the trace curve. Figure 4.10 shows a **Phong Antialias** rendering of the example.

Fourth example (Fig. 4.12)

In this example the **Type:** has been set to **Solid** in the tool's Element Selection box. Figure 4.11 shows the trace and section curves and Fig. 4.12 a **Phong Antialias** rendering of the solid when it has been created.

The Construct Offset Surface tool

Fig. 4.13 The **Construct Offset Surface** tool icon

This tool is for offsetting already constructed surfaces. In the tool's Element Selection box, the distance for the offsetting can be *entered* and also whether a copy of the original surface is to be retained. In the given example, the check box against **Copy** has been set on (**X** in check box).

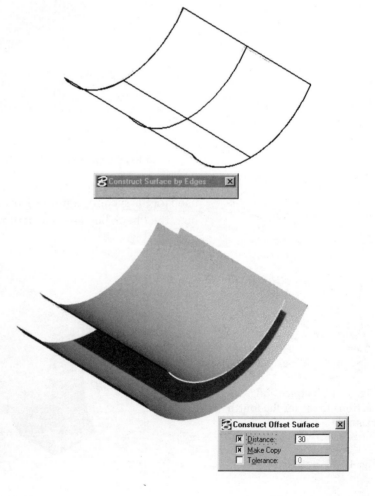

Fig. 4.14 The surface from which an offset is to be formed

Fig. 4.15 Example of the use of the **Construct Offset Surface** tool

Example (Fig. 4.15)

Figure 4.14 shows the original surface from which the offset surface was obtained. It has been constructed with the aid of the **Construct Surface by Edges** tool. Figure 4.15 is a **Phong Antialias** rendering of the two surfaces resulting from the offset – both the original and the offset surfaces.

Call the tool and the Status bar prompts are:

> **Construct Offset Surface > Identify surface** *pick* the already constructed surface.
>
> **Construct Offset Surface > Accept/Reject** *left-click* to accept.

The offset surface forms (Fig. 4.15).

Exercises

1. Figure 4.16 shows the sequence in four view windows for the construction of the surface shown in the rendering Fig. 4.17. The

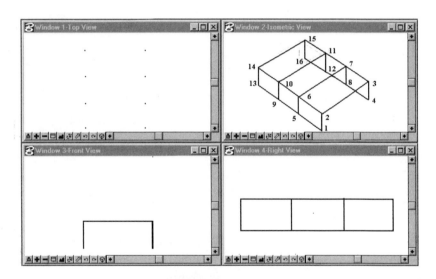

Fig. 4.16 The construction points for Exercise 1

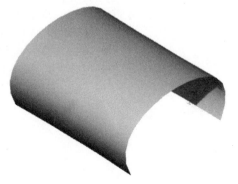

Fig. 4.17 Exercise 1

numbering of the sequence is given in the **Isometric view** window of Fig. 4.16. Construct the surface working to any convenient sizes. Note the B-spline curved surface resulting from the selection of the points during the construction.

2. Working to the dimensions given in Fig. 4.18 construct the surface shown in the rendering Fig. 4.19. The two section curves are 300 mm apart.

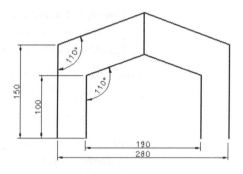

Fig. 4.18 Dimensions for Exercise 2

Fig. 4.19 Exercise 2

3. Working to the dimensions given in Fig. 4.20 construct the surface, a rendering of which is given in Fig. 4.21. The height of the surface is 25 mm.

4. Construct the outline Fig. 4.22 with the aid of the **Place Smart Line** tool. Copy it 250 mm from the original and construct a surface from the two outlines. Then offset the resulting surface by 20 mm and render – Fig. 4.23.

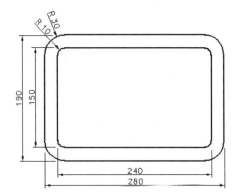

Fig. 4.20 Dimensions for
Exercise 3

Fig. 4.21 Exercise 3

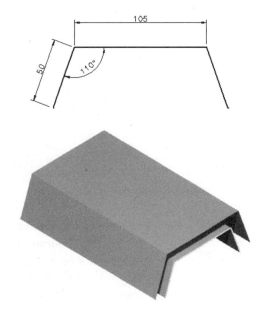

Fig. 4.22 Dimensions for
Exercise 4

Fig. 4.23 Exercise 4

CHAPTER 5

Customising a toolbox

Introduction

For the purpose of describing the customisation of a toolbox we will place the Boolean operators in a toolbox. In a standard MicroStation set-up there is no toolbox for these tools. They are for forming a union from surfaces (adding together), for forming a difference between surfaces (subtracting one from another) or forming intersections between surfaces (the parts where one surface intersects another).

To make up a new toolbox use **Customize** from the **Workspace** pull-down menu (Fig. 5.1). Otherwise, each time one of the operators is to be used, it must be *keyed-in* into the **Key in** window. *Keying-in* is carried out by first pressing the **Esc** key of the keyboard, which brings a small vertical line flashing cursor showing in the Key in window, followed by *entering* the letters of the command into the Key in window. Figure 5.2 shows the Boolean operator **union** so *keyed-in*. In fact for each of the Boolean operatives, it is only necessary to *key-in* the first two letters of each word of the command, with a space between each word. As each pair of letters is *keyed*, followed by a space, the full word appears in the Key in window:

For **Boolean surface union** – *key-in* bo su un.
For **Boolean surface difference** – *key-in* bo su di.
For **Boolean surface intersection** – *key-in* bo su in.

Fig. 5.1 Selecting **Customize** from the **Workspace** pull-down menu

Fig. 5.2 The Key in window with the Boolean surface union command *keyed-in*

Customising a toolbox for the Boolean operators

1. *Left-click* on **Customize** in the **Workspace** pull-down menu (Fig. 5.1). The **Customize** dialogue box appears (Fig. 5.3).
2. *Left-click* on the **Insert...** button. The **Modify Tool** dialogue box appears (Fig. 5.4). The dialogue box includes a number of tools which can be used to create an icon on the grid of the box. In the

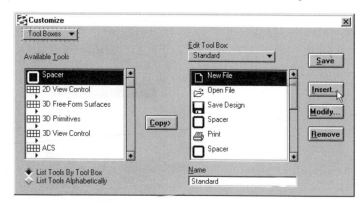

Fig. 5.3 The **Customize** dialogue box

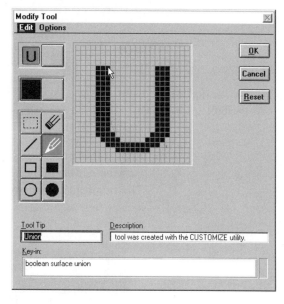

Fig. 5.4 Constructing an icon in the **Modify Tool** dialogue box

example in Fig. 5.4, a **U** for **Boolean surface union** has been constructed by *clicking* on grid squares with the pencil tool of the dialogue box.

3. In the dialogue box *enter* **boolean surface union** in the **Key-in** window and in the **Tool Tip** window *enter* **Union**. *Left-click* on the **OK** button. The icon appears in the **Customize** dialogue box.

4. In the **Customize** dialogue box, *left-click* on **Create Toolbox** in the **Edit Toolbox** pop-up list (Fig. 5.5). The **Create Toolbox** dialogue box appears (Fig. 5.6), followed by a *left-click* on the **OK** button.

5. The **Customize** dialogue box reappears, with the name **Boolean** in the **Edit Toolbox** window. *Left-click* on the **List Tools Alphabetically** icon at the bottom left-hand corner of the dialogue box and from **Available Tools** list, *left-click* on the **Union** icon in the list, followed by another *left-click* on the **Copy** button of the dialogue box. The icon appears in the **Boolean** list of icons.

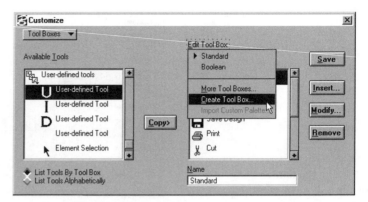

Fig. 5.5 Calling the **Create Toolbox**

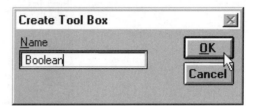

Fig. 5.6 *Enter* **Boolean** as the name for the new toolbox

6. Repeat this procedure for two further icons – a second for **Boolean surface difference** and a third for **Boolean surface intersection**. The result is as shown in Fig. 5.7.

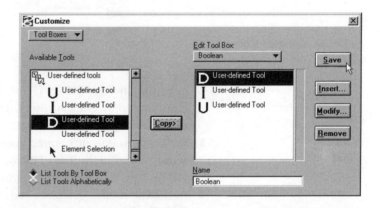

Fig. 5.7 Copying the three new icons to the **Boolean Toolbox** list

7. *Left-click* on the **Save** button. The **Boolean** toolbox has been created and saved.
8. Now *left-click* on **Toolboxes...** in the **Tools** pull-down menu (Fig. 5.8) and in the **Toolboxes** dialogue box (Fig. 5.9) *Left-click* on **Boolean**, followed by another *left-click* on the **OK** button. The newly created **Boolean** toolbox appears on screen (Fig. 5.10).

Fig. 5.8 Select **Toolboxes...** from the **Tools** pull-down menu

Fig. 5.9 Select **Boolean** from the **Toolboxes** dialogue box

Fig. 5.10 The newly created **Boolean** toolbox

Notes

1. The reader can construct any of his/her own toolboxes to include any tools which will be in constant use when constructing drawings. My **Boolean** toolbox is merely an example of the method used to create new toolboxes.
2. There is no reason why the reader should create such a toolbox. Because the Boolean operators will not be used all that often, the names (or abbreviations) of the Boolean operatives can be *keyed-in*. Remember, first press the **Esc** key, then *key-in* letters bo space su space, then either un (union) di (difference) or in (interference).

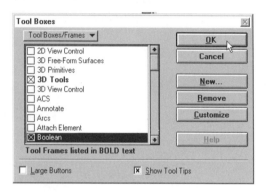

How to use the Boolean operators

The Change Surface Normal tool

It is important to ensure that the surface normals of surfaces being acted upon by the Boolean operators are set correctly. This is carried out by the **Change Surface Normal** tool from the **Modify 3D Surfaces** toolbox. To use the tool:

1. Hold a *left-click* on the **Trim Surface** tool icon in the **3D Tools** toolbox and the **Modify 3D Surfaces** flyout appears (Fig. 5.11).
2. *Drag* the flyout away from the toolbox and it changes to the **Modify 3D Surfaces** toolbox (Fig. 5.12).

Fig. 5.11 The flyout from **Trim Surface**

Fig. 5.12 The **Modify 3D Surfaces** toolbox

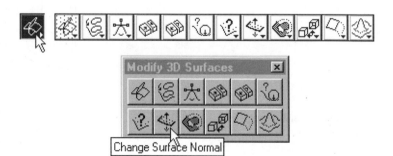

Fig. 5.13 The icon of the
Change Surface Normal tool

3. *Left-click* on the **Change Surface Normal** tool (Fig. 5.13).

Example of changing surface normals

Figure 5.14 shows two elliptical surfaces of projection. Call the
Change Surface Normal tool and *pick* the outline of the vertical
surface. The normals of the surface show as ghosted arrows facing
outwards from the surface. As this is the position required, *right-
click* to accept the direction of the normals. If you wished to change
their direction a *left-click* will change them to inward facing arrows.

Figure 5.15 shows the same operation carried out on the horizontal
surface. Again the direction of the normals was accepted with a
right-click.

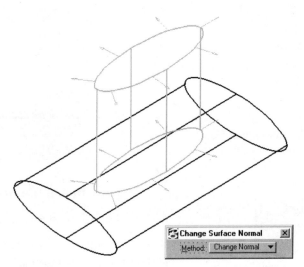

Fig. 5.14 The normals of a
surface showing in ghosted
form

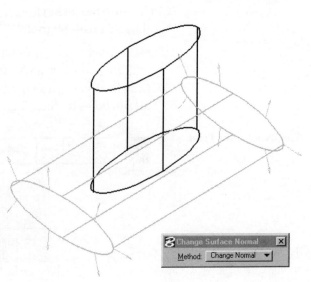

Fig. 5.15 The outward facing
normals for the horizontal
surface

Examples of using the Boolean operators

For the three examples following, two elliptical surface of projection, one vertical, the other horizontal, will be used. The two surfaces are shown in a four-window MicroStation 95 window in Fig. 5.16.

For each example the normals of both surfaces must be facing outwards. If they are not they should be changed with the aid of the **Change Surface Normal** tool.

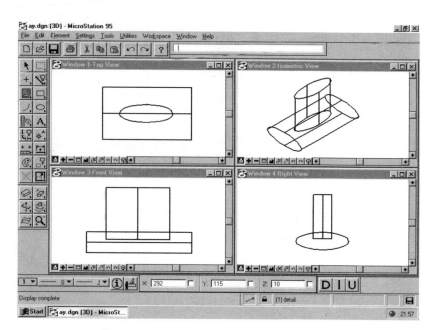

Fig. 5.16 The two elliptical surfaces of projection for the Boolean examples

First example – Union (Fig. 5.17)

Pick first on the vertical surface. The normals show. If outward facing, *pick* the horizontal surface. If the normals are also outward facing *left-click* and the union operation commences. It will take some time. When complete, the union ghosts. If correct *left-click* to accept. If incorrect *right-click* to reject. If it is incorrect, it is possibly due to the surface normals pointing the wrong way. Figure 5.17 shows the resulting MicroStation 95 four-window screen after the union has been rendered in the **Isometric View** window.

Second example – Difference (Fig. 5.18)

Figure 5.18 shows a **Phong Antialias** rendering of the effect of using the Boolean difference operator on the two surfaces. Again the normals must be outward facing on both surfaces. The horizontal surface must be *picked* first for the result shown in Fig. 5.18.

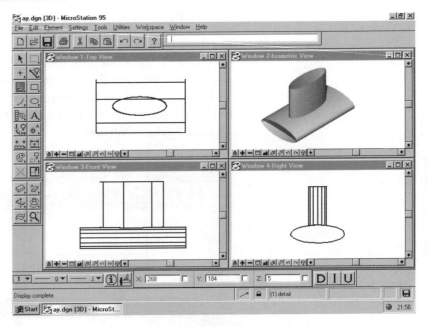

Fig. 5.17 First example

Fig. 5.18 Second example

Third example – Intersection (Fig. 5.19)

Figure 5.19 shows a **Phong Antialias** rendering of the effect of using the Boolean intersection operator on the two surfaces. Again the normals must be outward facing on both surfaces.

Fig. 5.19 Third example

Exercises

Caution

Two of the following exercises suggest the customisation of toolboxes. Be careful that you delete any toolbox which you customise when you have completed each exercise, unless you are the only person to use the computer at which you are working. **BUT** be careful when you delete either a tool icon or a toolbox that you are not deleting one of the toolboxes which are part of the MicroStation 95 system – it is easily done and unless you are very conversant with the resident toolboxes of MicroStation 95 and their icons such a deletion may be difficult for you to restore.

1. Customise a toolbox which you name **My Toolbox** and in which you include the following tools:

    Place Line, Place Arc, Place Circle, Place Block, Copy, Move, Place Text, Place Fence, Delete Element.

2. Open the **Modify Tool** dialogue box and design and construct an icon in the box which you think would be more suitable for the tool to operate **Boolean surface union** than that shown in this chapter.

3. Practise using the Boolean operators on simple surfaces of projection – e.g. a vertical hexagonal prism fitting into a horizontal cylinder; a vertical cylinder fitting into a horizontal square prism; a vertical cylinder fitting into a horizontal elliptical surface of projection.

CHAPTER 6

The 3D Primitives toolbox

Introduction

The **3D Primitives** toolbox contains six tools for the construction of 3D geometrical solids or surfaces in the form of prisms (slabs), spheres, cylinders, cones, torii or arc-style wedges. Figure 6.1 shows the flyout resulting from holding a *left-click* on the **Place Slab** tool icon in the **3D Tools** toolbox. Figure 6.2 shows the **3D Primitives** resulting from *dragging* the flyout away from the **3D Tools** toolbox and Fig. 6.3 shows the **3D Primitives** toolbox with the names of the tools in the toolbox.

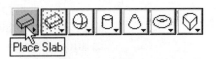

Fig. 6.1 The **3D Primitives** flyout

Fig. 6.2 The **3D Primitives** toolbox

Fig. 6.3 The names of the tools in the **3D Primitives** toolbox

With all the six tools in the toolbox, except for the **Sphere** tool, the **Type:** of 3D model can be set to be either surface or solid. In all the examples shown in this chapter the **Axis:** will be with the use of **AccuDraw**. The other **Axis:** methods of **Screen X (Y** or **Z)** or **Drawing X (Y** or **Z)** will not be shown here, but the reader is advised to practise drawing solids or surfaces after selecting these axis methods.

AccuDraw

It is assumed the reader will be acquainted with the use of AccuDraw. The following details should be noted:

1. When AccuDraw is in action pressing the **Space** key of the keyboard changes the AccuDraw **X**, **Y** and **Z** coordinate three-windows box to showing **Distance** and **Angle** two-windows box.

2. Pressing the **Tab** key switches between the AccuDraw **X**, **Y** and **Z** coordinate windows or between the **Distance/Angle** windows if they are in action.

3. When a small vertical blinking line cursor is showing in one of the AccuDraw windows, figures of dimension (length or angle) can be *entered* in that window to determine the size in the direction indicated – X, Y or Z, or Distance or Angle.

4. Each of the Element Selection boxes for the **3D Primitives** set of tools include boxes into which dimensions can be *entered*. Such dimensions are only acted upon if the check box against the boxes contains an **X**. If the check boxes are empty, the dimensions of the geometrical models produced by the tools depends upon the movement of the **AccuDraw** compasses and/or dimensions *entered* in the AccuDraw boxes.

Examples of the use of the 3D Primitive tools

Work in either a two- or four-window screen. This allows a start to be made in constructing a primitive and if necessary continuing in another window. For example, when constructing a slab the Length and Width can be determined in the **Top View** window by movement of the AccuDraw compass with the height being determined in the **Isometric View** window or in the **Front View** window. Most primitives can be easily constructed in a two-window screen – **Top View** and **Isometric View**.

Illustrations of all the examples are shown in a **Filled Hidden Line** form of rendering. The rendering is achieved by selecting **Filled Hidden Line** from the **Render** sub-menu of the **Utilities** pull-down menu, followed by a *left-click* in the **Isometric View** window. The primitive renders.

The Place Slab tool

First example (upper part of Fig. 6.5)

Place Slab

Fig. 6.4 The **Place Slab** tool

1. *Left-click* on the **Place Slab** tool icon. Its Element Selection box appears.
2. Select **Surface** from the **Type:** pop-up list.
2. *Left-click* in all the check boxes to set them all on (**Xs** in boxes).
3. *Enter* 100 in the **Length** box; 60 in the **Width** box; 20 in the **Height** box.
4. The following prompts appearing in the Status bar:

Place Slab > Enter Start point *left-click* at a convenient point in the **Top View** window. The **AccuDraw** compass appears centred at the selected point.

Place Slab > Enter length *drag* the AccuDraw compass horizontally and *left-click*. A ghosted box appears of length and width of the dimensions *entered* in the Element Selection box. *Left-click*.

Place Slab > Enter width *drag* the AccuDraw compass vertically and *left-click*. A top view of the slab appears.

Place Slab > Enter height in the **Isometric View** window *drag* the AccuDraw compass vertically and *left-click*.

Right-click and the primitive is completed.

Select **Filled Hidden Line** and *left-click* in the **Isometric View** window. The slab renders.

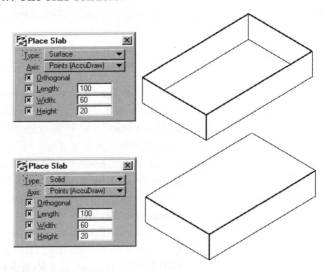

Fig. 6.5 First and second examples of **Place Slab**

Second example (lower part of Fig. 6.5)

Repeat as for the first example with **Type:** set to **Solid**.

Third example (Upper part of Fig. 6.6)

1. *Left-click* on the **Place Slab** tool icon. Its Element Selection box appears.
2. Select **Surface** from the **Type** pop-up list.
3. *Left-click* in the **Orthogonal** check box to turn **Orthogonal** off (no **X** in the check box).
4. *Enter* 100 in the **Length** box; 60 in the **Width** box; 20 in the **Height** box.
5. The following prompts appearing in the Status bar:

Place Slab > Enter Start point *left-click* at a convenient point in the **Top View** window. The **AccuDraw** compass appears centred at the selected point.

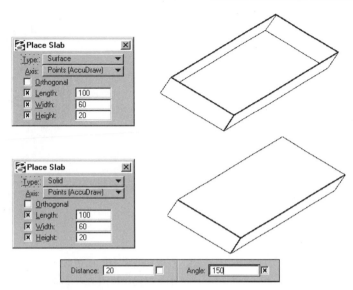

Fig. 6.6 Third and fourth examples of **Place Slab**

Place Slab > Enter length *drag* the AccuDraw compass horizontally and *left-click*. A ghosted box appears of length and width of the dimensions *entered* in the Element Selection box. *Left-click.*

Place Slab > Enter width *drag* the AccuDraw compass vertically and *left-click*. A top view of the slab appears.

Place Slab > Enter height press the **Space** key of the keyboard. The AccuDraw windows change to **Distance** and **Angle**. Press the **Tab** key. The **Angle** window becomes active (blinking cursor). *Enter* 150 in the **Angle** window. In the **Isometric View** window *drag* the AccuDraw compass vertically and *left-click*.

Right-click and the primitive is completed.

Select **Filled Hidden Line** and *left-click* in the **Isometric View** window. The slab renders.

Fourth example (lower part of Fig. 6.6)

Repeat as for the first example with **Type:** set to **Solid**.

The Place Sphere tool

Example (Fig. 6.8)

Fig. 6.7 The **Place Sphere** tool icon

1. *Left-click* on the **Place Sphere** tool icon (Fig. 6.7). Its Element Selection box appears.

2. *Left-click* in the **Radius** check box to set radius on. *Enter* 40 in the **Radius** box.

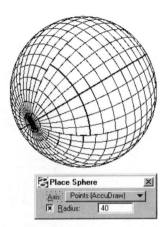

Fig. 6.8 The example of **Place Sphere**

3. *Left-click* in any window. *Drag* the AccuDraw compass in any direction and *left-click*. The sphere appears.
4. *Right click* to complete. Render with **Filled Hidden Line**.

The Place Cylinder tool

First example (upper part of Fig. 6.10)

1. *Left-click* on the **Place Cylinder** tool (Fig. 6.9). Its Element Selection box appears.
2. In the Element Selection box set all check boxes on (**X**s in boxes).
3. Set the **Type:** to **Surface**. *Enter* 30 in the **Radius** box and 60 in the **Height** box.
4. *Left-click* in the **Top View** window. A rectangle appears of radius and height of the cylinder. This rectangle can be rotated around the AccuDraw compass. Select a suitable position for the cylinder – watch the **Isometric View** window in particular and *left-click*.
5. *Right-click* to complete. Render with **Filled Hidden Line**.

Fig. 6.9 The **Place Cylinder** tool icon

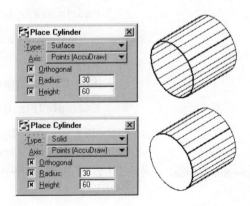

Fig. 6.10 First and second examples of **Place Cylinder**

Second example (lower part of Fig. 6.10)

Repeat as for the first example with **Type:** set to **Solid**.

Third example (upper part of Fig. 6.11)

1. *Left-click* on the **Place Cylinder** tool icon. Its Element Selection box appears.
2. In the Element Selection box *left-click* in the **Orthogonal** check box to turn it off (no X in the check box).
2. Select **Solid** from the **Type:** pop-up list.
3. *Enter* 30 in the **Radius** box and 60 in the **Height** box.
4. *Left-click* in the **Top View** window. An angled outline appears showing the radius and height. The angles of the rectangle can be changed by rotation around the AccuDraw compass.
5. Press the **Space** key. The AccuDraw window changes to **Distance** and **Angle**. Press the **Tab** key to make **Angle** active. Enter 45 in the **Angle** box and *left-click*. The angled cylinder appears.
6. *Right-click* to complete. Render with **Filled Hidden Line**.

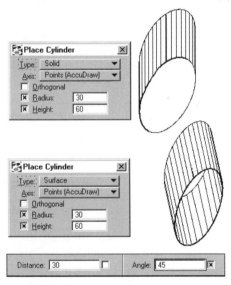

Fig. 6.11 Third and fourth examples of **Place Cylinder**

Fourth example (lower part of Fig. 6.11)

Repeat as for the third example with **Type:** set to **Surface**.

The Place Cone tool

First example (Fig. 6.13)

Fig. 6.12 The **Place Cone** tool icon

1. *Left-click* on the **Place Cone** tool icon (Fig. 6.12). Its Element Selection box appears.

2. In the Element Selection box set all check boxes on (**Xs** in boxes).
3. Set the **Type:** to **Surface**. *Enter* 20 in the **Top Radius** box; 50 in the **Base Radius** box; 75 in the **Height** box.
4. *Left-click* in the **Top View** window. An outline appears showing the top diameter, base diameter and height of the cone. This outline can be rotated around the AccuDraw compass. Select a suitable position for the cylinder – watch the **Isometric View** window in particular and *left-click*.
5. *Right-click* to complete. Render with **Filled Hidden Line**.

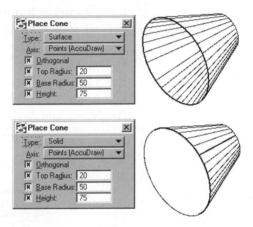

Fig. 6.13 First and second examples of **Place Cone**

Second example (lower part of Fig. 6.13)

Repeat as for the third example with **Type:** set to **Solid**.

The Place Torus tool

First example (upper part of Fig. 6.15)

Fig. 6.14 The **Place Torus** tool icon

1. *Left-click* on the **Place Torus** tool icon (Fig. 6.14). Its Element Selection box appears.
2. In the Element Selection box set **Type:** to **Solid**. Set all the check boxes on (**Xs** in the check boxes).
3. In the **Primary Radius** box *enter* 60. In the **Secondary Radius** box *enter* 10. In the **Angle** box enter 360.
4. Follow the prompts in the Status bar:

Place Torus > Enter start point *left-click* at a suitable point in a window. A ghosted line appears which can be rotated around the AccuDraw compass.
Place Torus > Define center point *drag* the line around until a suitable angle has been found and *left-click*. The torus appears.
Place Torus > Define axis of revolution *left-click*.

5. *Right-click* and the torus is completed. Render with **Filled Hidden Line**.

Second example (middle part of Fig. 6.15)

Repeat as for the first example with **Type:** set to **Surface** and with **Angle** set to 180.

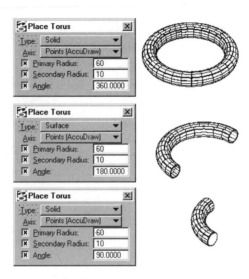

Fig. 6.15 First, second and third examples of **Place Torus**

Third example (lower part of Fig. 6.15)

Repeat as for the first example with **Type:** set to **Solid** with **Angle** set to 90.

The Place Wedge tool

First example (upper part of Fig. 6.17)

Fig. 6.16 The **Place Wedge** tool icon

1. *Left-click* on the **Place Wedge** tool icon (Fig. 6.16). Its Element Selection box appears.
2. In the Element Selection box set **Type:** to **Surface**. Set all check boxes on (**X**s in the check boxes).
3. *Enter* 50 in the **Radius** box; 180 in the **Angle** box; 20 in the **Height** box.
4. Following the prompts at the Status bar:

   Place Wedge > Enter start point *left-click* at a suitable point. A ghosted line appears which can be rotated around the AccuDraw compass.
   Place Wedge > Define center point *left-click* at a suitable point in the rotation.

Place Wedge > Define angle *left-click* (it has already been defined in the Element Selection box).

Place Wedge > Define height *left-click* (it has already been defined in the Element Selection box).

5. *Right-click* and the wedge forms. Render with **Filled Hidden Line**.

Second example (lower part of Fig. 6.17)

Repeat as for the first example with **Type:** set to **Solid** and with **Angle** set to 45.

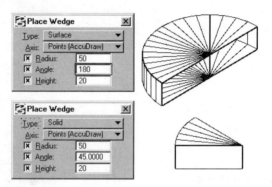

Fig. 6.17 First and second examples of **Place Wedge**

Notes

1. If settings for dimensions are not made in the Element Selection boxes of any of the **3D Primitive** tools, they can be set by *entering* figures in the respective **X**, **Y** and **Z** or in the **Distance** and **Angle** boxes of the **AccuDraw** windows as construction of the primitives proceeds. Remember to use the **Space** and **Tab** keys to move between the AccuDraw boxes.
2. Once again the reader is advised to practise with the **Screen X, Y** and **Z** and **Drawing X, Y** and **Z** options in the type: pop-up lists of the Element Selection boxes.
3. Start points for any of the primitive constructions can be *keyed-in* at the **Key in** window at the top of the MicroStation 95 window.

Exercises

Notes

1. Dimensions not included with the illustrations are left to your own judgement, but try to obtain good proportions with your answers.
2. All the drawings have been rendered with **Phong Antialias**. If you use this tool straight from the **Render** sub-menu of the **Utilities** pull-down menu without first setting the **Global Lighting** parameters

from the **Render** sub-menu of the **Settings** pull-down menu, you may find the renderings somewhat darker than those shown in the illustrations here.

3. Your answers can be rendered with the **Filled Hidden Line** tool from **Utilities/Render** if you do not wish to use **Phong Antialias**.

4. Renderings, including the **Global Lighting** settings, are described in Chapter 15.

5. For most of these exercises it will be sufficient to work in a two-window screen – **Top View** and **Isometric View**. It may be necessary to open other windows at times – e.g. **Front View** or **Right View** windows. It may be necessary to use the **Move** tool in any window to position a surface or a primitive exactly as desired. Remember to turn off **ACS Lock** from **Settings/Locks** before you attempt moving parts of your models. Failure to do so will make attempts at moving a part vertically (in the **Z** direction) impossible.

The following exercises are a mixture of surfaces and solids constructed with both **3D Primitive** and **3D Free-form Surfaces** tools.

1. Working to the dimensions and suggestions given with the rendering in Fig. 6.18, construct and render the model shown.

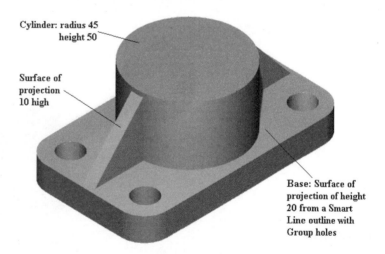

Cylinder: radius 45
height 50

Surface of
projection
10 high

Base: Surface of
projection of height
20 from a Smart
Line outline with
Group holes

Fig. 6.18 Exercise 1

2. Figure 6.19 shows a rendering of a 3D model of part of a braking device. Working to any suitable sizes, construct a similar 3D model and complete it by rendering.

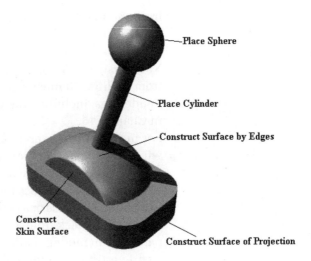

Fig. 6.19 Exercise 2

Place Sphere

Place Cylinder

Construct Surface by Edges

Construct Surface of Projection

Construct Skin Surface

3. Figure 6.20 shows a rendering of a 3D model for a tightening wrench from a tool holder for a lathe.

   Working to the suggested sizes given with the rendering, construct a similar 3D model and complete it by rendering either with **Phong Antialias** or with **Filled Hidden Line**.

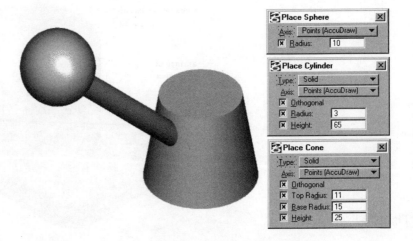

Fig. 6.20 Exercise 3

4. Working to the sizes suggested with the rendering, construct the 3D model shown in Fig. 6.21. Then render with **Phong Antialias** or with **Filled Hidden Line**.

5. Construct the 3D model shown in Fig. 6.22. Render with either **Phong Antialias** or with **filled Hidden Line**.

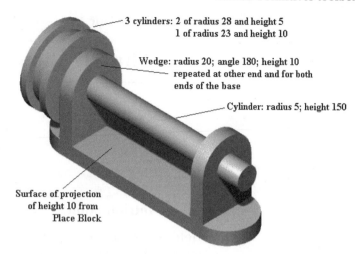

3 cylinders: 2 of radius 28 and height 5
1 of radius 23 and height 10

Wedge: radius 20; angle 180; height 10
repeated at other end and for both
ends of the base

Cylinder: radius 5; height 150

Surface of projection
of height 10 from
Place Block

Fig. 6.21 Exercise 4

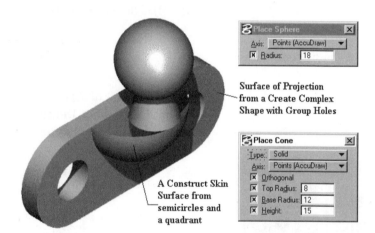

Surface of Projection
from a Create Complex
Shape with Group Holes

A Construct Skin
Surface from
semicircles and
a quadrant

Fig. 6.22 Exercise 5

CHAPTER 7

The 3D View Control toolbox

Fig. 7.1 The **Zoom In/Out** tool icon

Fig. 7.2 The **3D View Control** flyout

Introduction

Hold a *left-click* on the **Zoom In/Out** tool icon in the **3D Tools** toolbox (Fig. 7.1) and the **3D View Control** flyout appears (Fig. 7.2). *Drag* the flyout out onto the screen to see the **3D View Control** box (Fig. 7.3). The names of the tools in the toolbox are given in Fig. 7.4.

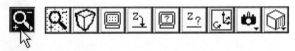

The examples of 3D solids given throughout this book do not rely upon either **Display Depth** or **Active Depth**. Because of this, the descriptions in this chapter are somewhat limited.

Fig. 7.3 The **3D View Control** toolbox

Fig. 7.4 The names of the tools in the **3D View Control** toolbox

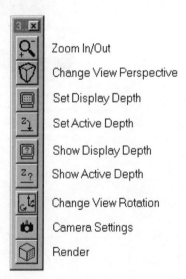

Zoom In/Out

Change View Perspective

Set Display Depth

Set Active Depth

Show Display Depth

Show Active Depth

Change View Rotation

Camera Settings

Render

The Zoom In/Out tool

Left-click on the tool. The following prompts appear at the Status bar:

Zoom > Enter zoom center point *left-click* at a suitable point.

Zoom > Define volume of interest a box appears, the size of which is under the control of the mouse. Move the mouse and the box changes size. When the area to be zoom is covered by the box, *left-click*.

Zoom > Define new volume move the mouse. The original box ghosts and a new box appears the size of which is under mouse control. Make the box smaller and the 3D model on screen reduces in size. Make the box bigger than the ghosted box and the 3D model enlarges. When satisfied *left-click*.

Display complete.

The Change View Perspective tool

Left-click on the tool icon (Fig. 7.5). The Status bar prompts show:

Fig. 7.5 The **Change View Perspective** tool icon

Change View Perspective > Select view *left-click* in the window in which the view is to be changed – normally the **Isometric View** window. A isometric box appears, or if in another window the box conforms to the shape of the window.

Change View Perspective > Define new perspective angle move the mouse and the box changes shape to a perspective outline which can be varied according to the mouse movement. When satisfied with the perspective as shown by the box, *left-click*.

Display complete.

Figure 7.6 shows a rendered example of a 3D model which was changed to a perspective view by the tool. Figure 7.7 shows the screen in which the change was made.

Fig. 7.6 An example of a perspective view formed from an isometric view with **Change View Perspective** tool

Display Depth

Four of the tools from the **3D View Control** toolbox are concerned with display depth – **Set Display Depth, Set Active Depth, Show**

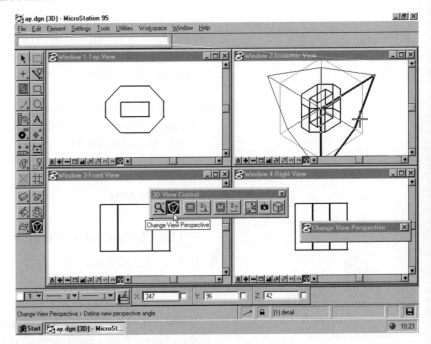

Fig. 7.7 A screen showing the action of the **Change View Perspective** tool

Display Depth and **Show Active Depth**. The display depth is the volume in the Z direction within which a 3D model is constructed. As far as the examples given throughout this book are concerned the setting of the display depth is not important. All the models described in the book can be constructed without the use of any of these tools. However, there are occasions when using the tool to set the display depth may prove to be of value and a single example follows to show how the display depth is set, how to use the active depth and how to show the display and active depths.

The Set Display Depth tool

Fig. 7.8 The **Set Display Depth** tool icon

1. In the **Top View** window, draw an ellipse with the aid of **Place Ellipse**.

2. Call the **Set Display Depth** tool (Fig. 7.8). The prompts in the Status bar show:

   Set Display Depth > Define front clipping plane *left-click* in the **Top View** window. A broken line outline showing the display depth appears in all windows. In the **Right View** window, *drag* the cursor vertically upwards to the position required for the front clipping plane. When satisfied *left-click* (Fig. 7.9).

3. The prompt changes to:

   Set Display Depth > Define back clipping plane still in the **Right**

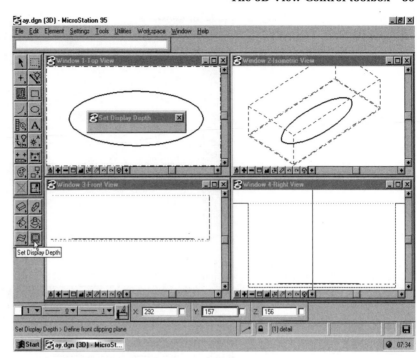

Fig. 7.9 Setting the front clipping plane

View window *drag* the cursor downwards onto the view of the ellipse edge. *Left-click*.
Display complete.

The Set Active Depth tool

Fig. 7.10 The **Set Active Depth** tool icon

Unless the active depth is set, any constructions will still be on the same plane as the already drawn ellipse. To set an active display depth, call the **Set Active Depth** tool (Fig. 7.10). The prompt in the Status bar becomes:

Set Active Depth > Enter active depth point *left-click* in the **Top View** window. Broken line outlines of the display depth appear in each of the view windows. In the **Right View** window *drag* the cursor vertically upwards to the point where the display depth is to be set (Fig. 7.11). *Left-click* and the active display depth is set.

The example of using the active depth settings

1. Having set the active depth, in the **Top View** window construct a circle with the **Place Circle** tool. The circle will appear on the active depth plane as shown in Fig. 7.12.
2. Call the **Construct Surface by Section** tool and form a surface from the ellipse and circle. The result is shown in a filled hidden line rendering in Fig. 7.13.

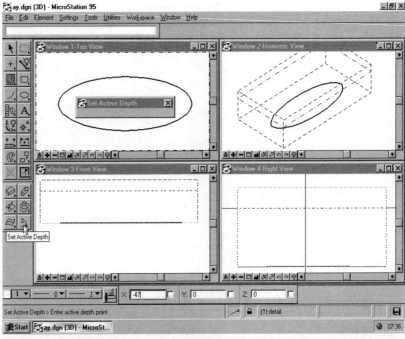

Fig. 7.11 Setting the active
display depth

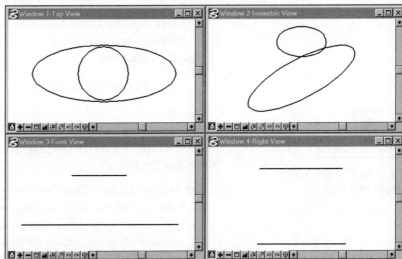

Fig. 7.12 A circle constructed
on the new active depth plane

Notes

1. The **front clipping plane** is the top (in the Z direction) of the display
   area.
2. The **back clipping plane** is the bottom (in the Z direction) of the
   display area.
3. The display depth can be set by *keying-in* figures in the **Key in**
   window in the form:

   dp=150,400

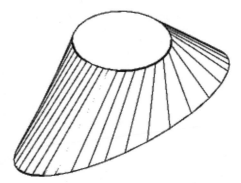

Fig. 7.13 The example of the
use of display depth and
active depth

4. The active depth can be set by *keying-in* in the **Key in** window in
   the form:

   az=300

The Show Display Depth tool

Call the tool (see Fig. 7.4). The prompt at the Status bar requests:

> **Show Display Depth > Select view** *left-click* in any view window
> and the positions of the display depth clipping planes shows
> in the Status bar in the form:
> **View 4: Display Depth= 200,300**

The Show Active Depth tool

Call the tool (see Fig. 7.4). The prompt at the Status bar requests:

> **Show Active Depth > Select view** *left-click* in any view window
> and the positions of the display depth clipping planes shows
> in the Status bar in the form:
> **View 4: Active Depth= 300**

The Change View Rotation tool

1. Construct a simple 3D solid such as that shown in Fig. 7.14.
2. *Left-click* on the **Change View Rotation** tool icon (Fig. 7.15). The
   View Rotation dialogue box appears showing an isometric block
   together with X,Y and Z axes. The axes include + and – points.
   Move the cursor onto one of the + or – points and hold down one
   of the mouse buttons. The isometric block rotates in response,
   allowing new positions in all coordinate directions. When satisfied
   that the block reflects the required rotation, *left-click* on the **Apply**
   button and the view in the **Isometric** window responds. Figs 7.16
   and 7.17 show examples of the use of this tool.

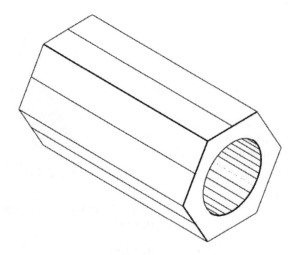

Fig. 7.14 The 3D solid for the **Change View Rotation** example

Fig. 7.15 The **Change View Rotation** tool icon

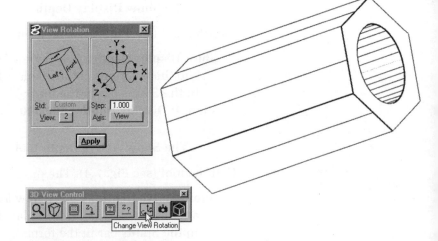

Fig. 7.16 An example of the use of the **Change View Rotation** tool

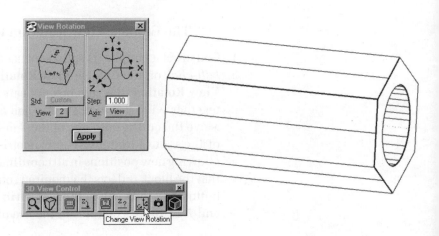

Fig. 7.17 Another example of the use of the **Change View Rotation** tool

The Camera Settings tool

The settings required for this tool will be described in Chapter 15.

The Render tool

Fig. 7.18 The **Render** tool icon

A number of illustrations in earlier chapters have included renderings – both of the **Filled Hidden Line** and of the **Phong Antialias** types. Renderings will be described more fully in Chapter 15.

When the **Render** tool is selected (Fig. 7.18), its Element Selection box includes three pop-up lists – **Target:**, **Shading Mode:** and **Shading Type:**. Figure 7.19 shows the lower of these three pop-up lists and their contents.

More is given about the various forms of rendering in Chapter 15. However, as renderings have been included in earlier chapters, the reader may like to experiment with the various forms of rendering available through selection from the options available in the tool's Element Selection box.

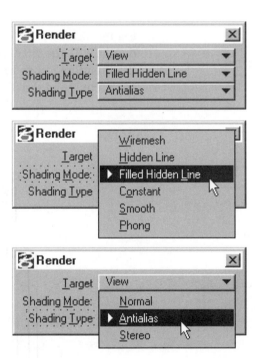

Fig. 7.19 The **Render** Element Selection box and two of its pop-up lists

Exercises

Three exercises will be sufficient to allow experimentation with the tools in the **3D View Control** dialogue box. When attempting these exercises use your own judgement about sizes.

1. Figure 7.20 shows a rendering of a 3D model constructed with the aid of the **Construct Surface by Section** tool on two active display depths and then rendered with **Phong Antialias**.

   Working to suitable sizes, construct the 3D model.

Fig. 7.20 Exercise 1

2. Figure 7.21 shows a 3D model constructed on several active display depths with the aid of the **Construct Surface of Projection** tool and then rendered with **Filled Hidden Line**. Working to any suitable sizes, construct the 3D model shown.

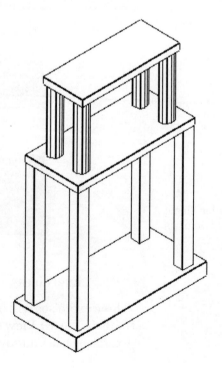

Fig. 7.21 Exercise 2

3. Figure 7.22 is the 3D model constructed in answer to Exercise 2 and then acted upon with the **Change View Perspectives** tool.

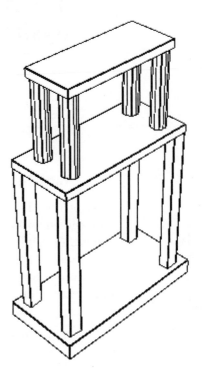

Fig. 7.22 Exercise 3

CHAPTER 8

The Auxiliary Coordinate System (ACS)

Introduction

Most of the 3D models shown in the pages of this book can be constructed without using the Auxiliary Coordinate System (ACS). The rather brief description in this chapter is therefore merely an introduction to this system, by which X, Y planes which are at angles to the top, front, right, left and back window planes can be set to allow construction at angles to the planes as set in the windows.

The ACS toolbox

To call the toolbox onto the screen, *left-click* on **Auxiliary Coordinates** in the **Tools** pull-down menu (Fig. 8.1) and the toolbox (Fig. 8.2) appears. The names of the tools in the toolbox are given in Fig. 8.3.

If the operator is intending using the **ACS** tools to any extent the toolbox can be *dragged* to the bottom of the MicroStation 95 window as shown in Fig. 8.4.

A number of different auxiliary coordinate systems can be set up and saved with names *entered* in the **Auxiliary Coordinate Systems** dialogue box (Fig. 8.5), called with a *left-click* on **Auxiliary Coordinates** in the **Utilities** pull-down menu (Fig. 8.6).

Fig. 8.1 Calling the **ACS** toolbox to screen

Fig. 8.2 The **ACS** toolbox

The ACS tools

To demonstrate the effect of using the various tools in the **ACS** toolbox, first set **ACS Triads** in the **View Attributes** dialogue box on in all windows by calling the dialogue box onto screen from the **Settings** pull-down menu. Then in the **Top View** window draw a

Define ACS (Aligned with Element)

Define ACS (By Points)

Define ACS (Aligned with View)

Rotate Active ACS

Move ACS

Select ACS

Fig. 8.3 The tools in the **ACS** toolbox

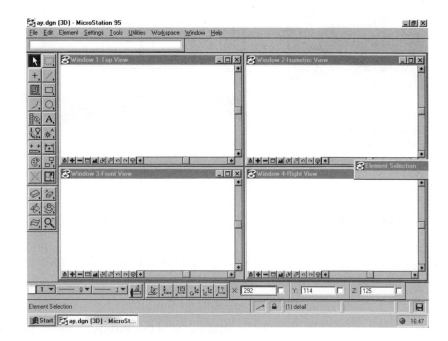

Fig. 8.4 The **ACS** toolbox *dragged* to the bottom of the MicroStation 95 window

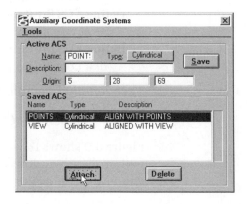

Fig. 8.5 The **Auxiliary Coordinate Systems** dialogue box

Fig. 8.6 Calling the **Auxiliary Coordinate Systems** dialogue box to screen

Fig. 8.7 Using the **Define ACS (Aligned with Element)** tool

rectangle of any size with the aid of the **Place Block** tool. Use **Fit View** in each window to bring the triads and the rectangle centrally in each window.

The Define ACS (Aligned with Element) tool

Figure 8.7 shows the result of *picking* an element in the **Front View** window in response to the prompts appearing at the Status bar when the tool is called. The **ACS Triads** in each window show the position of the auxiliary plane resulting from *picking* the element.

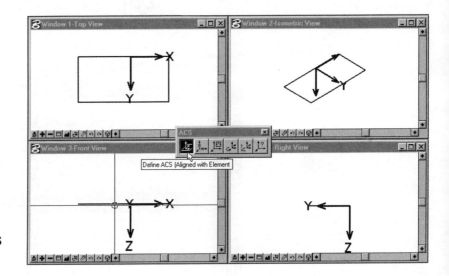

The Define ACS (by Points) tool

Figure 8.8 shows the effect of selecting three points in response to prompts in the Status bar when this tool is called:

> **Define ACS (by Points) > Enter first point @x axis origin** *pick* a point or *key-in* a coordinate point in the **Key in** window.
> **Define ACS (by Points) > Enter second point on x axis** *pick* a point or *key-in* a coordinate point in the **Key in** window.
> **Define ACS (by Points) > Enter point on y axis** *pick* a point or *key-in* a coordinate point in the **Key in** window.

Then *left-click* completes the setting.

The Define ACS (Aligned with View) tool

Figure 8.9 shows the results of selecting this tool. To align the ACS with a view window, call the tool and *left-click* in the required window. In the example given in Fig. 8.9, the **Top View** window has

Plate I A model
constructed on a single
level and rendered in an
assigned material

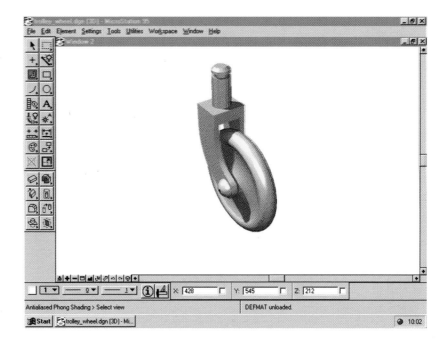

Plate II The rendered
model shown in Plate I
with the **Define Materials**
dialogue box open

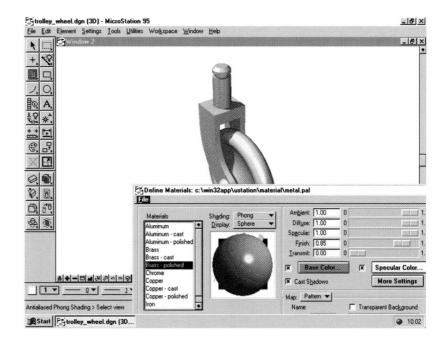

Plate III   The model shown in Plate I with materials assigned to each of the three levels on which the model was constructed

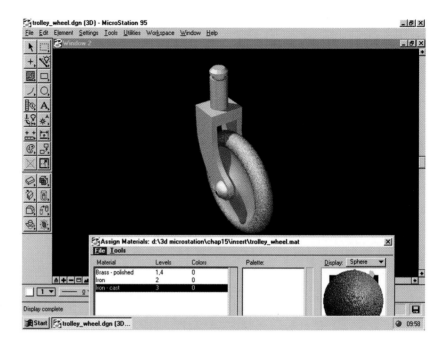

Plate IV   A model displayed in four view windows; the isometric view has been rendered

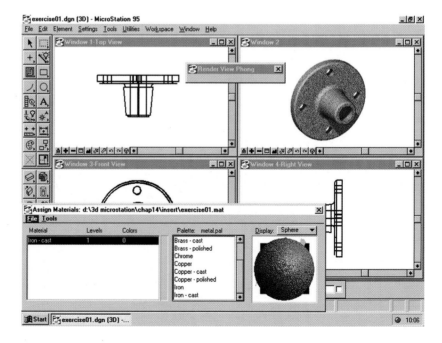

Plate V A 3D model rendered with a single material assigned to all parts

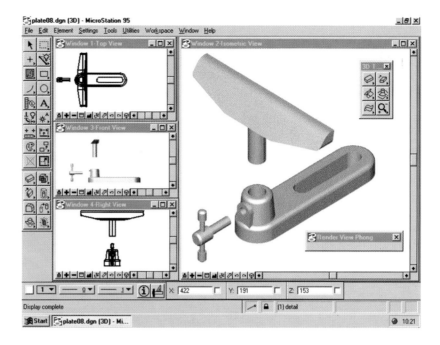

Plate VI The model shown in Plate V rendered with materials assigned on three levels and displayed on a black background

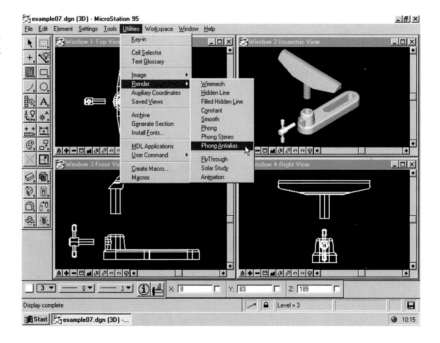

Plate VII A model rendered in isometric view with the same material assigned to all levels

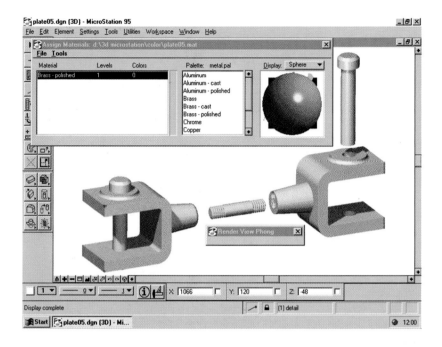

Plate VIII The same model shown in Plate VII but with different materials assigned to all four levels on which the model was constructed

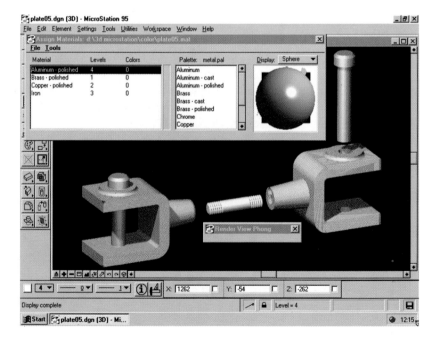

Plate IX A model rendered using global lighting and with no assigned material

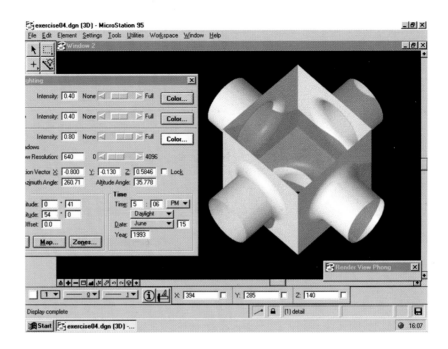

Plate X Copies of a model constructed on two levels, each with a different material assigned to the base of the model

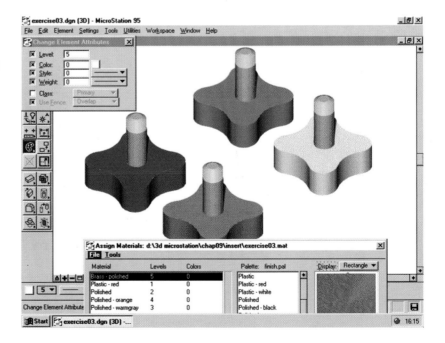

Plate XI A model
displayed in three
windows and rendered
using the material **Brass -
polished**

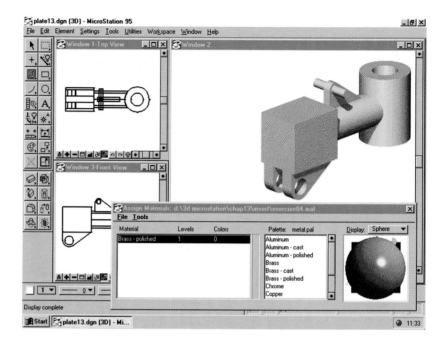

Plate XII A model
rendered using certain
global lighting settings
and with an assigned
material

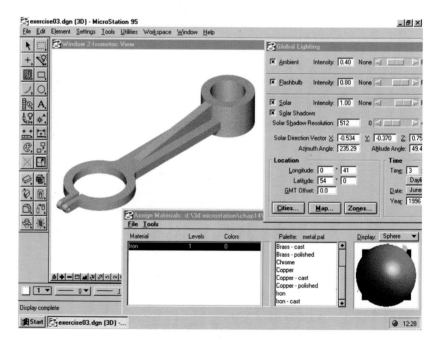

Plate XIII A model rendered after being assigned materials on three levels

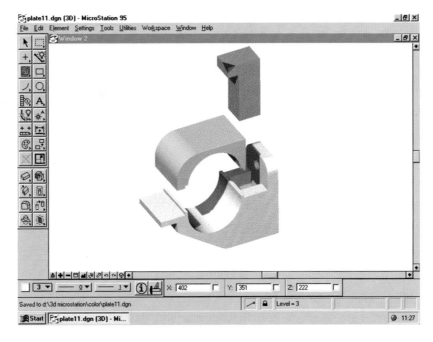

Plate XIV A model rendered with two assigned materials

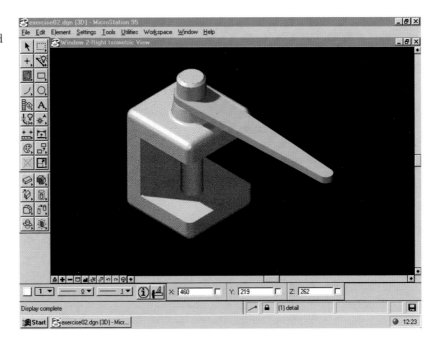

Plate XV A model
showing the effects of
changing the global
lighting colours

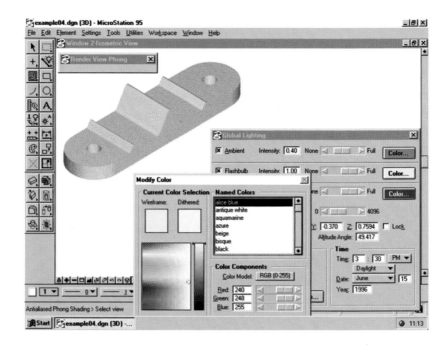

Plate XVI A model
rendered using an added
spotlight

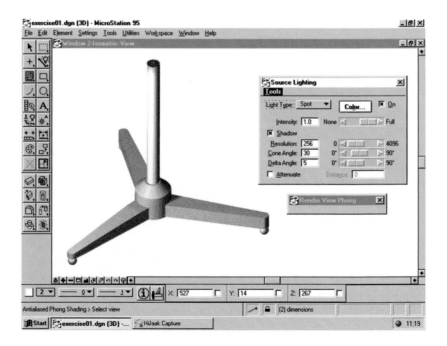

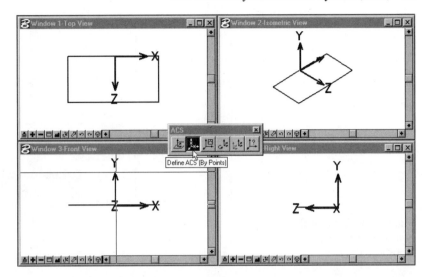

Fig. 8.8 Using the **Define ACS (by Points)** tool

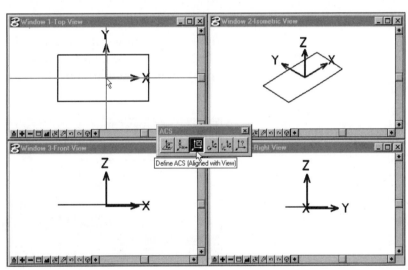

Fig. 8.9 Using the **Define ACS (Aligned with View)** tool

been selected. Note that the other windows conform to the setting in the selected view window.

The Rotate Active ACS tool

First example of Rotate Active ACS

Figure 8.10 shows the **Rotate Active ACS** dialogue box appearing when the tool is selected. In this illustration all **Rotate:** angles (X, Y and Z) are set to 0°. A *left-click* on the **Absolute** button, followed by another on the **Done** button and the windows are set to the required ACS, which in this example is the default setting when MicroStation 95 is started.

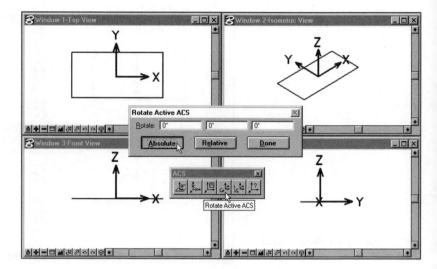

Fig. 8.10 First example. The results of *entering* zeros in the **Rotate:** windows

Second example of Rotate Active ACS

Figure 8.11 shows the results of *entering* 45° in the **Rotate:** X window, followed by *left-clicks* on the **Absolute** and **Done** buttons. The ACS is rotated around the X axis by 45°.

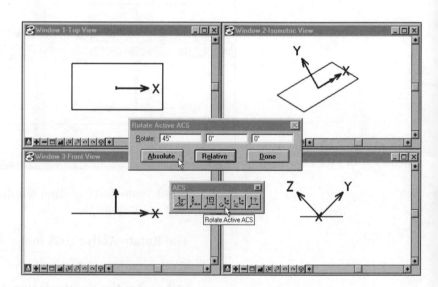

Fig. 8.11 Second example. The results of *entering* 45 in the **Rotate:** X window

Third example of Rotate Active ACS

Figure 8.12 shows the results of *entering* 45° in the **Rotate:** Y window, followed by *left-clicks* on **Absolute** and **Done** buttons. The ACS is rotated around the Y axis by 45°.

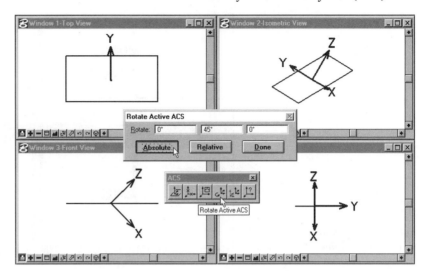

Fig. 8.12 Third example. The results of *entering* 45 in the **Rotate:** Y window

Fourth example of Rotate Active ACS

Figure 8.13 shows the results of *entering* 45° in the **Rotate:** Z window, followed by *left-clicks* on **Absolute** and **Done** buttons. The ACS is rotated around the Z axis by 45°.

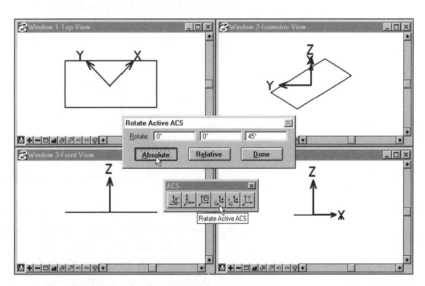

Fig. 8.13 Fourth example. The results of *entering* 45 in the **Rotate:** Z window

The Select ACS tool

When this tool is selected the names of the various auxiliary coordinate systems saved in the **Auxiliary Coordinate Systems** dialogue box appear with their ACS triads in the view windows. Figure 8.14 shows the results when the tool is selected after the two systems saved as shown in Fig. 8.5 have been saved. A left-click on either name (or its triad) brings the selected ACS back to screen.

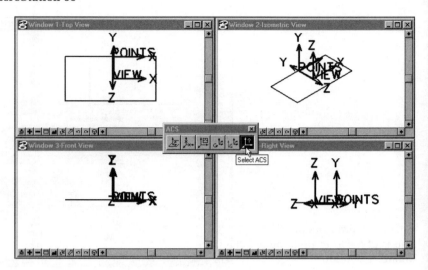

Fig. 8.14 The result of selecting the **Select ACS** tool

An example of the use of Auxiliary Coordinate Systems

1. In the **Settings** pull-down menu select **View Attributes** and make **ACS Triads** active for all windows.
2. In the **Top View** window construct Fig. 8.15.

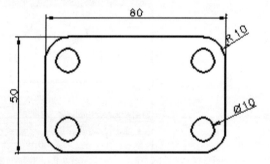

Fig. 8.15 Example – the drawing in the **Top View** window

3. Using the **Group Hole** tool make a group of the drawing.
4. Form a solid by projection of the drawing 20 high.
5. Using **Rotate Active ACS** set to rotation of 45 in Y.
6. Set the **ACS Lock** on (**X** in its check box) and draw a circle of diameter 20 on the new ACS.
7. Using **Rotate Active ACS** set to rotation of 135 in Y.
8. Draw a circle of diameter 20 on the new ACS.
9. Form solids of projection from both solids each 60 high.
10. Turn the **ACS Lock** off (no **X** in its check box).
11. Turn AccuDraw off (press the **Q** key with the AccuDraw compass on screen. The compass disappears as does the AccuDraw window).
12. Move both cylinders to suitable positions (Fig. 8.16).

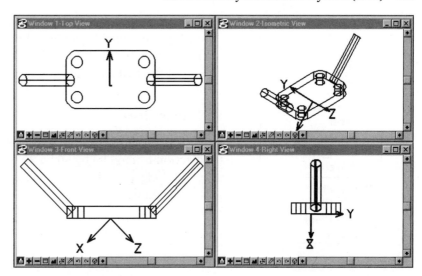

Fig. 8.16 Example. Cylinders moved to suitable positions

13. Make the **isometric View** window full size, call the **Change View Perspective** tool and change the isometric view of the 3D model to a perspective view with its aid.
14. Render the model – preferably with the aid of **Phong Antialias** as shown in Fig. 8.17.

Fig. 8.17 the 3D model after rendering

Notes

1. It is thought that sufficient information has been included in this chapter to allow the reader to experiment further with the **ACS** tools.
2. As can be seen in the illustrations showing the effects of using the **ACS** tools, in all cases, providing the triads are showing, the directions of the X, Y and Z axes are changed to conform to the selected ACS.

Full
Toggles
☐ A**x**is
☐ **G**rid
☐ **U**nit
☐ A**s**sociation
☐ **L**evel
☐ G**r**aphic Group
☐ Text **N**ode
☐ **I**sometric
☒ **B**oresite
☒ **A**CS Plane
☐ ACS P**l**ane Snap
☐ **D**epth

🔒 (1) detail

Fig. 8.18 Setting the **ACS** lock on (**X** in check box)

3. In order to ensure that an element is actually drawn on a new **ACS**, the **ACS Lock** must be set on. This can be set either from the lock icon in the Status bar (Fig. 8.18) or by selection from the **Locks** submenu of the **Utilities** pull-down menu.

Exercises

1. Figure 8.19 shows a Phong Antialias rendering of a surface of projection formed 80 by 50 by 20 with two diameter 20 cylinders, each 50 long at angles of 45° centrally at each end. Construct the given 3D model.

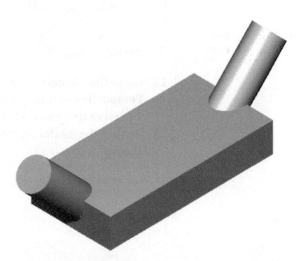

Fig. 8.19 Exercise 1

2. Figure 8.20 shows a Phong Antialias rendering of a vertical pipe of height 120 and of diameter 50 with walls 5 thick; another pipe, 100 long, of diameter 15 with walls 2 thick meets it at an angle of 45°, and a rectangular pipe 80 long with side lengths 60 by 40 meets at an angle of 60°.

   Construct the three pipes and render the resulting 3D model.

3. To construct the 3D model of a vase shown in Fig. 8.21, set the **Front View** window as an **ACS** with the X axis horizontal and the Y axis vertical. Then construct a surface of rotation to form the vase outline and a tubular surface to form the handle. Complete the 3D model by rendering. Work to any convenient sizes of your own choice.

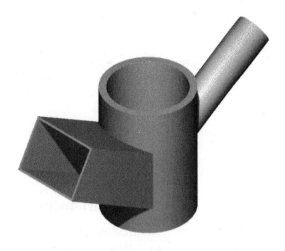

Fig. 8.20 Exercise 2

Fig. 8.21 Exercise 3

CHAPTER 9

AccuDraw

Introduction

AccuDraw, its compasses and its coordinate windows provide an excellent facility for producing accurate 3D models. The major feature of AccuDraw is its two compasses – The **Rectangular** AccuDraw compass (Fig. 9.1) and the **Polar** AccuDraw compass (Fig. 9.2).

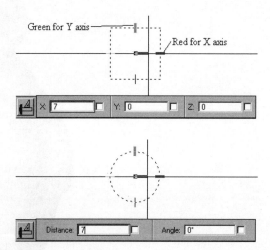

Fig. 9.1 The **Rectangular** AccuDraw compass with its corresponding AccuDraw coordinate window

Fig. 9.2 The **Polar** AccuDraw compass with its corresponding AccuDraw coordinate window

When the Rectangular compass is active, the AccuDraw coordinate window shows three coordinates **X**, **Y** and **Z**. When the Polar AccuDraw compass is active, the AccuDraw window shows **Distance** and **Angle**. Toggling between the two types of compass is carried out by pressing the **Space** key of the keyboard. If the Rectangular compass is showing, press the Space key and it changes to a Polar compass. If the Polar compass is showing, pressing the Space key changes the compass to the Rectangular type.

It will be seen from reference to Figs 9.1 and 9.2 that a thick bar shows the directions of the X and Y axes on both compasses. The default colours for these axis direction bars are as shown in Fig. 9.1. If desired their colours can be changed by first calling the **AccuDraw**

Settings dialogue box to screen as shown in Fig. 9.3 (**Settings** pull-down menu), then a *left-click* on either the **X axis...** or the **Y axis...** buttons brings up the **Modify Axis Color** dialogue box, from which other colours can be chosen. The axis colour bars are important because, no matter in which position the compass is placed, the operator can always readily determine which are the X and Y positive axis directions.

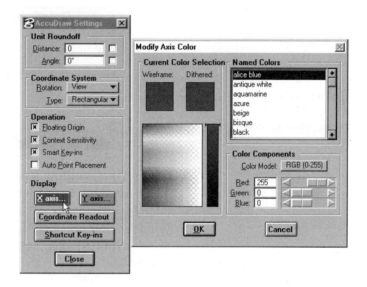

Fig. 9.3 Changing the AccuDraw X and Y axis bars

AccuDraw keyboard shortcuts

Another important feature of the AccuDraw system is the ease with which the direction of the compasses can be changed by pressing certain keyboard keys. The more important of these keyboard shortcuts are given below.

V In the window showing the AccuDraw compass **V** sets the compass axes to the view window in which the compass is acting. If the compass is already aligned correctly in the view window, it is not altered. Figure 9.4 shows the Rectangular

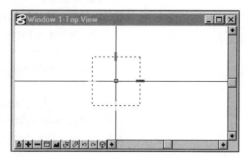

Fig. 9.4 The Rectangular compass in its **Top View** position

compass in the **Top View** window. The compass is in its normal top view position.

F In any view window **F** sets the AccuDraw compass to **Front View** axes. Figure 9.5 shows the compass in the **Top View** window after pressing the **F** key. The compass changes into its normal **Front View** window position, but in the **Top View** window.

Fig. 9.5 The Rectangular compass in the **Top View** window after pressing the **F** key

S In any view window **S** sets the AccuDraw compass to **Right View** axes, or **Left View** axes in the **Left View** window (Window 8). Figure 9.6 shows the compass in the **Top View** window after pressing the **S** key. The compass changes to its normal **Side** (Right or Left) view position, but in the **Top View** window.

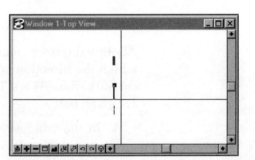

Fig. 9.6 The Rectangular compass in the **Top View** window after pressing the **S** key

T In any view window **T** sets the AccuDraw compass to **Top View** axes.

RQ allows the AccuDraw compass to be rotated freely by *dragging* with the mouse. Figure 9.7 shows the positions of the cursor cross hairs as the compass is *dragged* to a new rotation. When the compass is in a desired position, release the mouse key.

RX rotates the AccuDraw compass by 90° around the X axis.

RY rotates the AccuDraw compass by 90° around the Y axis.

RX rotates the AccuDraw compass by 90° around the Z axis.

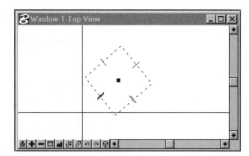

Fig. 9.7 Rotating the compass after pressing **R+Q** keys

RZ rotates the AccuDraw compass as defined by 3 points – X axis origin, X axis and Y axis. Figure 9.8 shows the broken line field resulting from choosing three points. The first selected point sets the centre of the compass. The second defines the end of the X axis. The third defines the end of the Y axis.

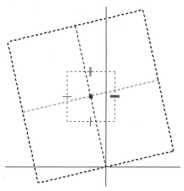

Fig. 9.8 Defining the position of the compass by the selection of three points

Other AccuDraw keyboard shortcuts

With an AccuDraw active on screen – i.e. call a tool and *left-click* in a view window – pressing the **R** key of the keyboard brings up the **AccuDraw Shortcuts** dialogue box (Fig. 9.9). Scroll through the shortcut details in this dialogue box to see other keyboard shortcuts available when working with AccuDraw.

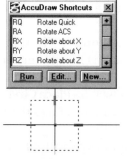

Fig. 9.9 The **AccuDraw Shortcuts** dialogue box

Using Tab and cursor keys

When working with AccuDraw, pressing the **Tab** key of the keyboard toggles between the coordinate boxes in the AccuDraw window. The same toggling can be carried out by using either of the up and down cursor keys. The **Tab** key is usually on the left-hand side of the keyboard and carries two arrows facing in opposite directions. The cursor keys are usually at the bottom right of the letter keys. Each carries an arrow. It is those with vertical arrows which can be used for this toggling.

3D models constructed with the aid of AccuDraw

First example

1. In the **Top View** window draw a circle of radius 40. In the other windows use **Fit View** to fit the outline into the areas of the windows and **Zoom Out** to set the outline to a manageable size.
2. With **Move Parallel** set to **Distance:** 5 and **Make Copy:** add an inner circle. With **Group Hole** form the two circles into a group.
3. With **Construct Surface of Projection** form an orthogonal solid from the group of height 150.
4. **Fit View** in each window.
5. Make sure the **ACS Plane** lock is off (no **X** in check box).
6. With the cursor in the **Front View** window select the **Place Circle** tool. The AccuDraw compass appears in the window. Press the **T** key. The compass changes to a top view position.
7. In the **Front View** window construct the outline shown in Fig. 9.10.

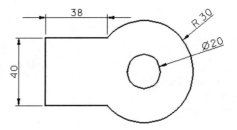

Fig. 9.10 The outline constructed in the **Front View** window

8. With **Construct Surface of Projection** create a solid from the outline of height 5.
9. Move the newly created part into position as shown in Fig. 9.11. Note that the scroll bars have been removed in this illustration for the sake of clarity.
10. With the cursor in the **Right View** window select the **Place Circle** tool. The AccuDraw compass appears in the window. Press the **S** key. The compass changes to a side view position.
11. Construct two circles as shown in Fig. 9.12. Form a group from the two circles.
12. With **Construct Surface of Projection** form a solid of height 50.
13. With **Move** move the solid into position as shown in Fig. 9.13. It may be necessary to use the **T**, **F** or **S** shortcuts to enable the move to be effective in the windows in which the move is being effected.
14. Two rendered views of the model are shown in Fig. 9.14.

Fig. 9.11 The newly created
solid after moving

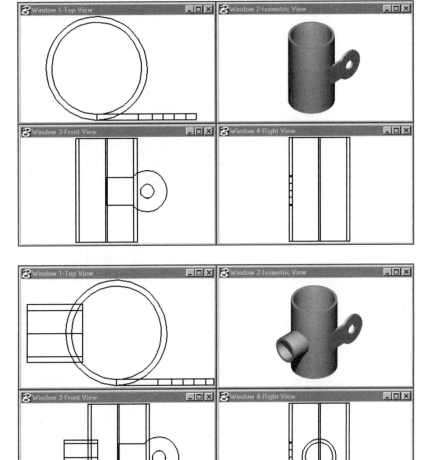

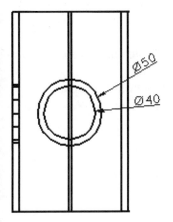

Fig. 9.12 Two circles in the
Right View window

Fig. 9.13 The completed 3D
model in four viewports

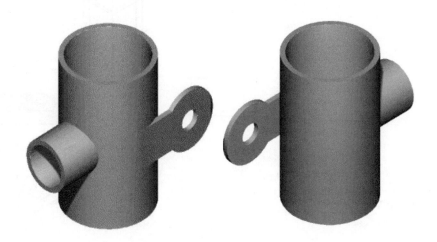

Fig. 9.14 Two rendered views
of the first example

Second example

This example will be constructed in the **Isometric View** window, except for the construction of a vertical square pipe.

1. In the **Top View** window draw a square of 40 mm sides with the aid of **Place Block**. **Move Parallel** a copy at 4 mm inside the square. Group the two blocks with **Group Hole**.
2. With the aid of **Construct Surface of Projection** create a square pipe of height 200 from the double square.
3. Enlarge the **Isometric View** window to whole screen size.
4. In the **Isometric View** window use **Fit View** and **Zoom Out** to obtain a reasonable size of model.

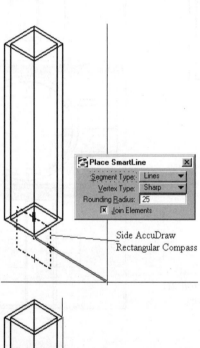

Fig. 9.15 Constructing part of the second example using the **Side View** AccuDraw compass

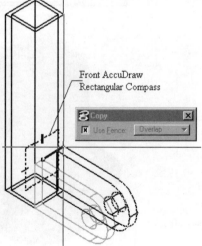

Fig. 9.16 Constructing part of the second example using the **Front View** AccuDraw compass

5. Select **Smart Line** and set its parameters in the Element Selection box to **Lines**, **Rounded**, **Rounding Radius** 25.

6. Set the **ACS Plane** lock on (**X** in its check box).

7. Using snap (*both-click*) at the nearest bottom corner, *pick* the snap point. Press the **S** key to set the AccuDraw compass to a side view position (Fig. 9.15). Draw a line in the X direction 100 long, in the Y direction 50 long and in the −X direction 100 long.

8. Reset the **Smart Line** Element Selection box to **Vertex Type** sharp and join the two ends of the first smart line with a new smart line.

9. Still in the side compass draw a hole at the centre of the 25 end of the smart line of radius 10. Use **Center** snap on the arc of radius 25 at the end of the smart line outline to accurately determine the position of the hole. Form a group with **Group Hole**.

10. With **Construct Surface of Projection** create a solid from the group of height 10.

11. Select **Copy**. *Both-click* (snap tentative point) at top right-hand corner of the new solid. Press key **F** and copy the solid through 30 mm along the +ve **X** axis (Fig. 9.16).

12. Select **Place Block**. Using the **Midpoint** snap, snap at the midpoint of the nearest line on the vertical pipe. Press the **T** key to place the AccuDraw compass in its top view position. Draw a block of 40 mm square (should just fit around the vertical pipe).

13. Using the **Center** snap draw a circle of radius 50 mm around the square block just drawn (Fig. 9.17).

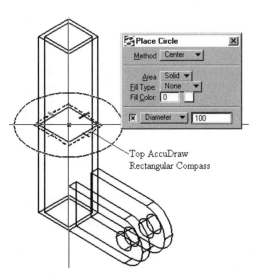

Fig. 9.17 Constructing part of the second example using the **Top View** AccuDraw compass

14. With **Group Hole** form the block and circle into a group. With **Construct Surface of Projection** create a solid of height 20.

15. Render with Filled Hidden line. The result will be as in Fig. 9.18.

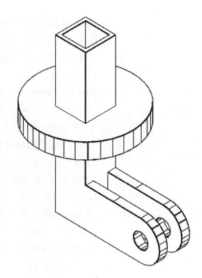

Fig. 9.18 A filled Hidden Line
rendering of the second
example

Note

Figures 9.15–9.17 show the positions of the AccuDraw Rectangular
compasses as each part of the 3D model was constructed.

Third example

1. In the **Front View** window construct the outline as shown in Fig.
   9.19. Form the outline into a group with **Create Complex Shape** and
   form the hole with **Group Hole**.

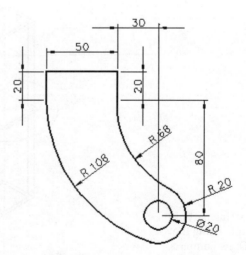

Fig. 9.19 Outline for first part
of the third example

2. With **Construct Surface of Projection** form the shape into a solid of
   height 10.

3. In the **Isometric View** window press the **F** key and **Copy** the solid through 60 mm in the X direction (Fig. 9.20).

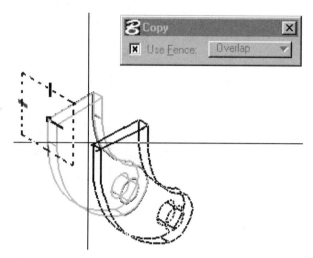

Fig. 9.20 Third example.
Copying through 60 mm

4. Press the **T** key, call the **Place Block** tool and with the aid of the **Keypoint** snap draw a block as shown in Fig. 9.21. With the **Surface of Projection** tool create a solid from the block 20 high.

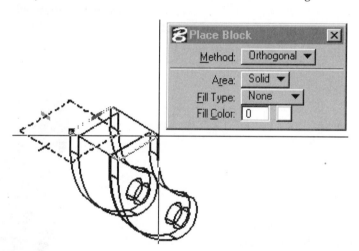

Fig. 9.21 Third example.
Drawing a block for the upper part

5. In the **Right View** window draw an outline of the spindle on which the wheel of the third example rotates (Fig. 9.22). With **Construct Surface of Revolution** form the outline into a solid through 360°.
6. Also in the **Right View** window construct an outline for the wheel (Fig. 9.23). With **Construct Surface of Revolution** form the outline into a solid through 360°.
7. Working in any window as may be necessary **Move** the spindle and wheel into their correct final position in the 3D model. Note – **ACS Lock** must be off to enable this to be carried out.

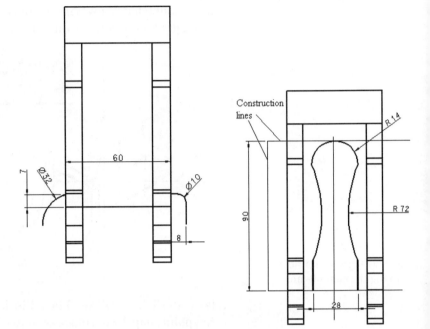

Fig. 9.22 Third example. The spindle outline

Fig. 9.23 Third example. Outline for the wheel

8. Make the **Isometric View** window fill the screen and, with the aid of **Phong Antialias** render the view. Figure 9.24 shows this rendering.

Fig. 9.24 Third example. A **Phong Antialias** rendering of the completed 3D model

9. With **Change View Rotation** amend the position of the 3D model on the screen. Render this new view as shown in Fig. 9.25.

Exercises

1. Figure 9.26 is a rendering of a 3D model of a door handle constructed to the dimensions given in Fig. 9.27.

Fig. 9.25 Third example. A rendering of the new view

Fig. 9.26 A rendering of Exercise 1

Fig. 9.27 A two-view first angle orthographic projection for Exercise 1

Construct the 3D model of the handle to the given sizes and render the completed model.

2. Figure 9.28 is a rendering of three-way connecting piece constructed from pipes of outside diameter 20 mm and inside diameter 8 mm, with 2 mm by 2 mm slots cut 4 mm from the ends of the connectors.

Construct a 3D model of the connector to these dimensions and render your completed model.

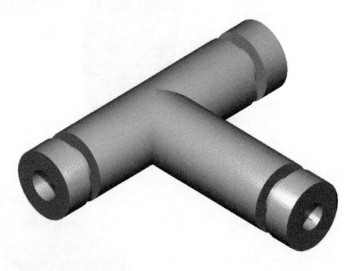

Fig. 9.28 Exercise 2

3. Figure 9.29 gives the dimensions for the construction of the 3D model shown rendered in Fig. 9.30.

Construct the given 3D model to the sizes given and when complete render the model.

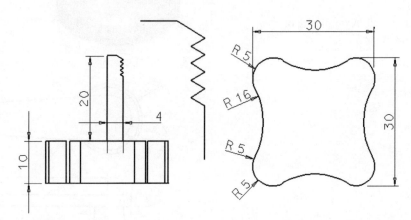

Fig. 9.29 Details of sizes for Exercise 3

Fig. 9.30 Exercise 3

4. Figure 9.31 is a rendering of a surface of projection formed from a **Smart Line**. The projection is 30 mm deep.
    Details of dimensions are given in Fig. 9.32.

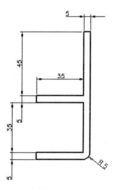

Fig. 9.31 Exercise 4

Fig. 9.32 Details of sizes for Exercise 4

5. Figure 9.33 is a rendering of the 3D model for this exercise. Figure 9.34 gives the dimensions to which the model was constructed. Construct and render the model.

Fig. 9.33 A rendering of
Exercise 5

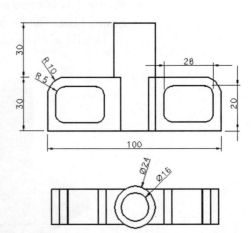

Fig. 9.34 Details of sizes for
Exercise 5

CHAPTER 10

The Modify 3D Surfaces toolbox

Introduction

The **Modify 3D Surfaces** toolbox contains a few tools the uses for which are beyond the scope of this introductory book, so some of the tools in this toolbox will not be described. The use of one of the tools tool – **Change Surface Normal** – has already been shown in Chapter 5. In previous chapters, even when some of the **Modify Surfaces** tools should have been used, their use has been ignored. If the reader has worked through examples in previous pages and saved the resulting drawings to file, he/she may care to reload them and use the **Modify Surfaces** tools to complete the model drawings.

To call the toolbox onto the MicroStation 95 window, hold a *left-click* on the **Trim Surfaces** tool icon in the **3D Tools** toolbox. The **Modify 3D Surfaces** flyout appears (Fig. 10.1). *Drag* the flyout on screen and the **3D Modify Surfaces** toolbox appears (Fig. 10.2).

The names of the tools are shown against a vertically placed toolbox in Fig. 10.3. To demonstrate the uses for most of the tools in the toolbox a number of examples follow.

Fig. 10.1 The flyout of the **3D Modify Surfaces** tools

Fig. 10.2 The **3D Modify Surfaces** toolbox

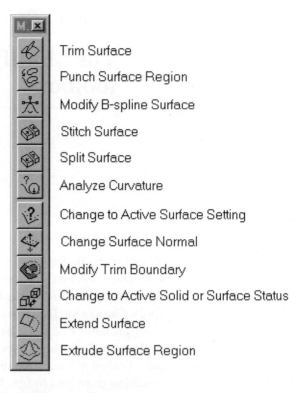

Fig. 10.3 The names of the **3D Modify Surfaces** tools

The Trim Surfaces tool

First example (Fig. 10.6)

Construct two surfaces of projection, one from a circle, the other from a block. The resulting **Isometric View** window of the two surfaces is shown in Fig. 10.4 in a **Phong Antialias** rendering.

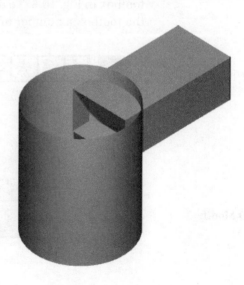

Fig. 10.4 First example. The two surfaces prior to trimming

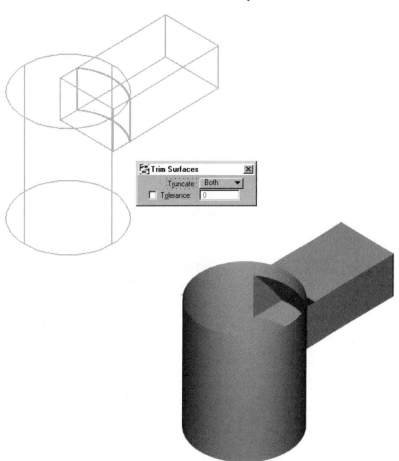

Fig. 10.5 First example. The ghosted appearance of the surfaces and intersection waiting to be accepted

Fig. 10.6 First example. The result of the trimming

When the tool is selected, the following prompts appear in the Status bar:

Trim Surfaces > Identify first surface *pick* the first surface.
Trim Surfaces > Identify second surface *pick* the other surface. the line of intersection between the two surfaces appears in ghosted form as shown in Fig. 10.5.
Trim Surfaces > Accept/Reject *left-click* to accept if the line of intersection appears to be correct. The resulting trimming is shown in Fig. 10.6 in a **Phong Antialias** rendering.

The completed drawing appears.

Notes

1. In this example settings in the Element Selection box are for **Truncate:** Both with a **Tolerance:** setting of 1. It is advisable to *enter* a number in the **Tolerance:** box to avoid a very long time elapsing

before the trimming takes place. The tolerance setting determines the sampling distance around the line of intersection.

2. Care must be taken in *picking* the parts of two surfaces. If *picked* in the wrong place the wrong parts of the surfaces may be trimmed.

Second example (Fig. 10.8)

In this example, a cylinder formed from a circle with **Construct Surface of Projection** has been trimmed to fit against a surface formed from two semicircles with the aid of **Construct Surface by Section**. The procedure for forming the trimming followed the same steps as for the first example. The semicircular surface was selected, followed by selecting the cylinder. In this example the **Tolerance:** setting was not involved.

Figure 10.7 shows the two surfaces prior to using the **Trim Surfaces** tool and Fig. 10.8 the resulting 3D model with both surfaces trimmed.

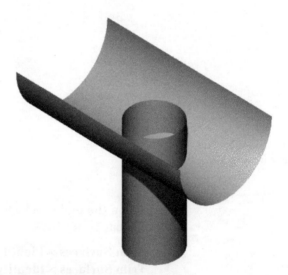

Fig. 10.7 Second example. The two surfaces prior to trimming

The Punch Surface Region tool

First example (Fig. 10.10)

This tool can be used to cut (punch) holes of any shape in existing surfaces. In this first example, a semicircular surface is to have a hexagonal hole punched through its surface as shown in the left-hand drawing of Fig. 10.9. When the tool is called, the Status bar shows the following prompts:

Punch Surface Region > Identify surface *Pick* the surface.
Punch Surface Region > Accept surface/Identify curve *Pick* the hexagon. An arrow appears showing the direction in which

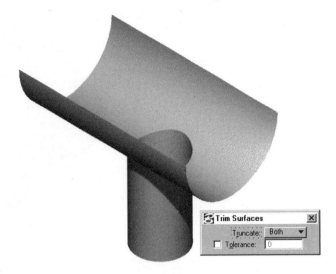

Fig. 10.8 Second example. The trimmed surfaces

the 'punching' is to take place (right-hand drawing of Fig. 10.9). If in the wrong direction select a different **Direction:** setting in the tool's Element Selection box and watch the arrow change.

Punch Surface Region > Accept curve *Left-click* and the punching takes place.

Figure 10.10 shows the results of the effect of the tool's action for the first example.

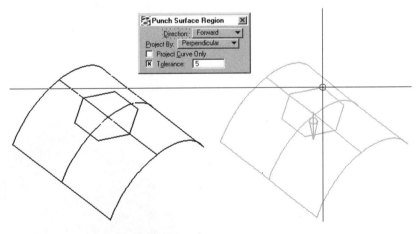

Fig. 10.9 First example. The surface and the curve and the ghosted drawing showing the direction arrow

Second example (Fig. 10.12)

In this example the same semicircular surface is to have an outline from a group made up from two circles and two lines trimmed to shape (Fig. 10.11). Construct the surface and draw the shape, then follow the same procedure as for the first example.

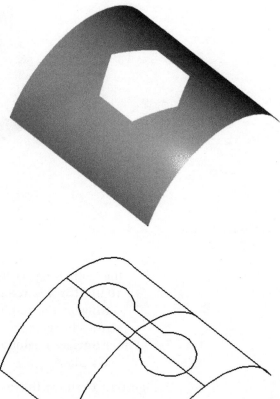

Fig. 10.10 First example. The
resulting 3D model

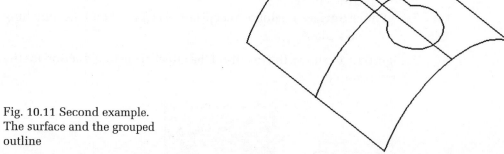

Fig. 10.11 Second example.
The surface and the grouped
outline

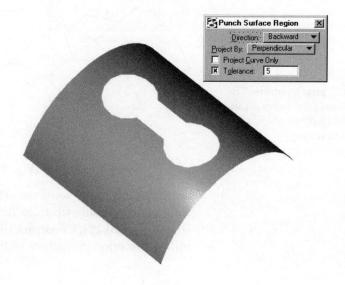

Fig. 10.12 Second example. A
Phong Antialias rendering of
the surface with its punched
hole

The Stitch Surface tool

In this single example of the use of this tool, two surfaces, one formed from arcs, the other from rounded Smart Lines as shown in Fig. 10.13, are stitched together with the aid of the tool. When the tool is called, the Status bar prompts are:

Stitch Surface > Identify first surface *Pick* one of the surfaces.
Stitch Surface > Identify first surface *Pick* the other surface.
Stitch Surface > Identify and Accept/Reject *Left-click.*

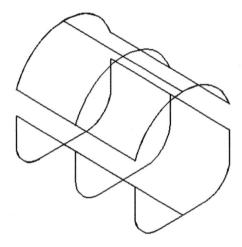

Fig. 10.13 The two surfaces to be stitched together

And the surfaces are stitched together as shown in Fig. 10.14. A **Phong Antialias** rendering of the example is given in Fig. 10.15.

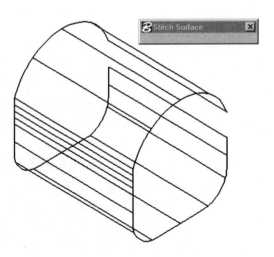

Fig. 10.14 The stitched model before rendering

Fig. 10.15 The stitched model after rendering

Note

Care must be taken as to the positions of the *pick* points when identifying the surfaces to be stitched together, otherwise the results may not be as desired. Some experimentation with positions of the identifying points is advisable.

The Split Surface tool

In this single example, a surface, formed from a pair of Smart Lines (left-hand drawing of Fig. 10.16), is split at its centre with the aid of the tool. When the tool is selected, the Status bar prompts are:

Split Surface > Identify surface *pick* the surface.

Split Surface > Select end pnt of partial delete *pick* the start point at the point where the split is to start.

Split surface > Select end pnt, or RESET to change direction either *pick* the end point of the split, or *right-click* which changes the direction along which the split will occur. If changing direction then a *left-click* at an end point determines the length of the split.

The right-hand drawing of Fig. 10.16 shows a split in the first direction, Fig. 10.17 the split in the changed direction.

The Modify Trim Boundary tool

If an error has been made in *picking* a side of a surface when trimming boundaries between surfaces with the **Trim Surfaces** tool, the error can be rectified with the aid of the **Modify Trim Boundary** tool. An example is given in Fig. 10.18, in which the left-hand

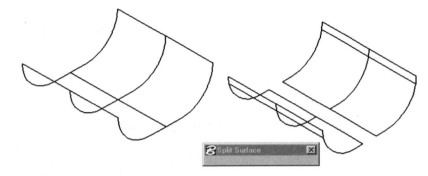

Fig. 10.16 Example of the use
of the **Split Surface** tool

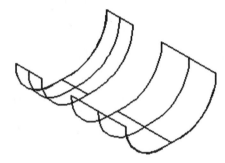

Fig. 10.17 The split in the
changed direction

rendering shows a trimmed pair of surfaces before modifying the
trim boundary and the right-hand rendering the same pair with the
modification. When the tool is called the Status bar prompts show:

> **Modify Trim Boundary > Identify element** *Pick* the surfaces with
> the trimmed boundary.
> **Modify Trim Boundary > Accept change bounds/Reject** If satisfied
> *left-click.*
> **Modify Trim Boundary > Identify element**.

The settings in the **Trim Boundary:** pop-up list in the tool's Element
Selection box affects the way in which the action of the tool takes

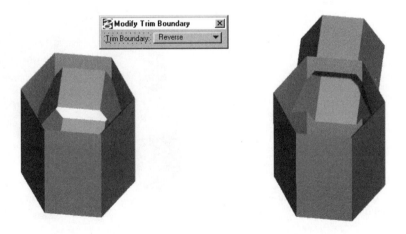

Fig. 10.18 An example of the
use of the **Modify Trim
Boundary** tool

place. The pop-up list shows three options – **Reverse** (as shown in Fig. 10.18), **Remove All** and **Remove One**.

The Change to Active Solid or Surface Status tool

Calling this tool brings the following prompts into the Status bar:

> **Change to Active Solid or Surface Status > Identify element** *pick* the surface or solid to be changed.
>
> **Change to Active Solid or Surface Status > Accept, change cap/ Reject** *left-click* if satisfied with the ghosted result or *right-click* to reject and revert to original status.

First example (Fig. 10.20)

Figure 10.19 shows a surface formed from a Smart Line outline with the aid of the **Construct Surface of Projection** tool. Figure 10.20

Fig. 10.19 First example – before change

Fig. 10.20 First example – after change

shows the same surface changed to a solid after being selected with the **Change to Active Solid or Surface Status** tool in action.

Second example (Fig. 10.22)

In this example the two hexagonal surfaces of projection have been changed to solids. Figure 10.21 shows the 3D model before the change and Fig. 10.22 the hexagonal surfaces changed to solids.

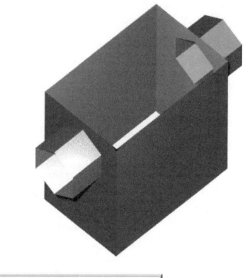

Fig. 10.21 Second example – before change

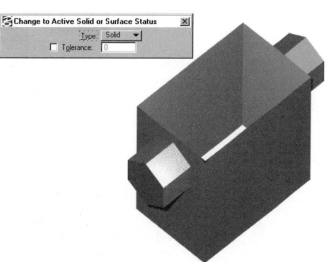

Fig. 10.22 Second example – after change

The Extend Surface tool

When the tool is called its Element Selection box shows a box labelled **Continuity:** the pop-up list for Continuity shows three options – **Position**, **Tangent** and **Curvature**. The three examples showing uses for this tool given below are based upon these three options.

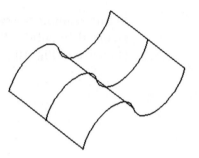

Fig. 10.23 The surface for the **Extend Surface** tool examples

First example (Fig. 10.24)

In this example, **Continuity** has been set to Tangent and the **Scale:** to 1, with the **Top View** AccuDraw compass operating.
When the tool is called the Status bar options are:

Extend Surface > Identify surface *pick* one of the straight edges of the surface.

Extend Surface > Accept/Reject *drag* the surface to its required extension and when satisfied *left-click* to accept.

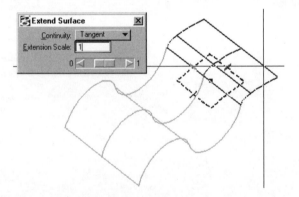

Fig. 10.24 First example

Second example (Fig. 10.25)

In this example, the **Continuity** setting has been changed to **Position** and the same method of *dragging* the curve to its new extension applies. There is no **Scale:** setting when using the **Position** option. Again the **Top** AccuDraw compass is in operation.

Third example (Fig. 10.26)

In this example, the **Continuity** setting has been changed to **Curvature** and the **Scale** to 0.5 and the same method of *dragging* the curve to

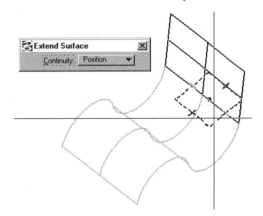

Fig. 10.25 Second example

its new extension applies. The **Front** AccuDraw compass is in operation.

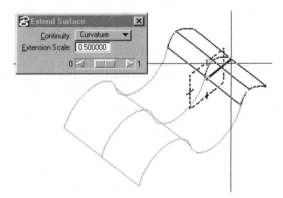

Fig. 10.26 Third example

Notes

1. If a part of the surface such as that shown in the above examples, other than a straight edge is *picked,* the resulting extensions will be different to those shown in the examples. The reader is advised to practise *picking* other parts of a surface.
2. Note however that if the surface is not a curved surface, such as that shown in Fig. 10.23, the options of continuity do not fully apply.

The Extrude Surface Region tool

Three examples are given with different settings in the tool's Element Selection box. The surface involved in each example is the same – one constructed from two arcs using the **Construct Surface by Section** tool (Fig. 10.27). The curve being extruded onto the surface is a circle. In each example note the settings in the tool's Element

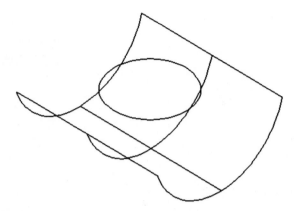

Fig. 10.27 The surface and curve for the three examples

Selection box given with the illustrations for each example. In the first two examples, after the action of the tool has taken place, the curve (circle) has been deleted in order to make the illustrations clearer. The results will be different with different positions of *picking* a point on the surface. In each example the Status bar prompts are the same:

Extrude Surface Region > Identify surface make settings in the Element Selection box then *pick* the surface.

Extrude Surface Region > Accept surface/Identify curve *pick* the curve – i.e. the circle.

First example (Fig. 10.28)

A **Phong Antialias** rendering of the resulting extrusion is given after the curve (circle) has been deleted. Note the settings in the Element Selection box.

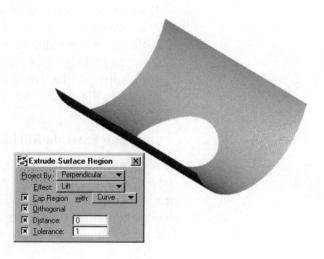

Fig. 10.28 First example

Second example (Fig. 10.29)

A **Phong Antialias** rendering of the resulting extrusion is given after the curve (circle) has been deleted. Again, note the settings in the Element Selection box.

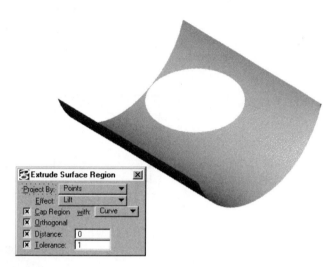

Fig. 10.29 Second example

Third example (Fig. 10.30)

This example is shown in its wireframe form to display the curve extruded onto the surface from the circle. Note also that the circle has not been deleted in this example. Again note the settings in the tool's Element Selection box.

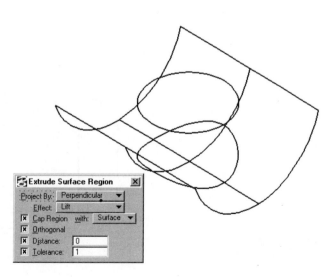

Fig. 10.30 Third example

Exercises

1. Figure 10.31 gives the dimensions of two intersecting surfaces formed with the aid of the **Construct Surface by Section** tool. Figure 10.32 is a **Phong Antialias** rendering of the solid completed by trimming the two surfaces with the aid of the **Trim Surfaces** tool. Construct the two surfaces and complete the exercise by trimming both surfaces to produce the required 3D model.

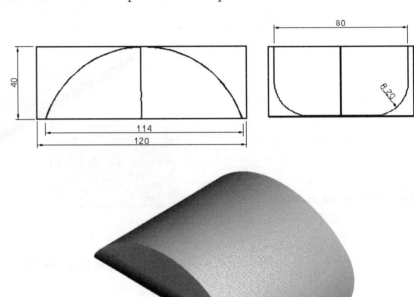

Fig. 10.31 Exercise 1. Dimensions

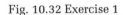

Fig. 10.32 Exercise 1

2. Figure 10.33 gives the dimensions of three curves which were used to form surfaces of revolution around a single central axis. Figure

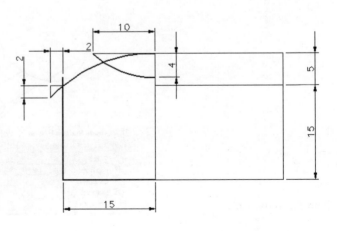

Fig. 10.33 Exercise 2. Dimensions

Fig. 10.34 Exercise 2

10.34 is a **Phong Antialias** rendering of the three surfaces after overlapping edges of the surfaces have been trimmed with the aid of **Trim Surface**. Construct and render the 3D model. Figure 10.35 shows the screen with four windows after the 3D model has been constructed.

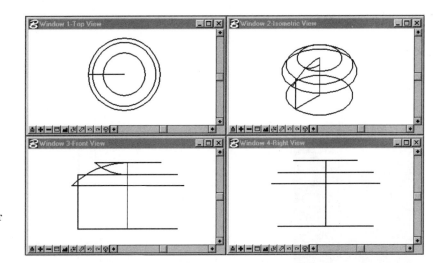

Fig. 10.35 Exercise 4. The four window screen when the exercise has been completed

3. Figure 10.36 is a rendering of a series of pipes formed with the aid of the **Construct Tubular Surface** tool. When the pipes had been formed, their intersections were trimmed with the aid of the **Trim Surface** tool. The outer pipe is of outer diameter 12 and inner 6, the uprights are of outer diameter 8 and inner 6. Construct the assembly of pipes, add a base and render.

4. The two illustrations Figs 10.38 and 10.39 give details for this exercise. Figure 10.37 shows the completed 3D model. Figure 10.38 gives the dimensions in an orthographic projection.

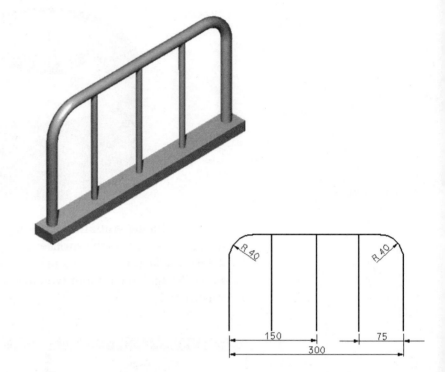

Fig. 10.36 Exercise 3

Fig. 10.37 Exercise 3.
Dimensions

Fig. 10.38 Exercise 4

Fig. 10.39 Exercise 4.
Dimensions

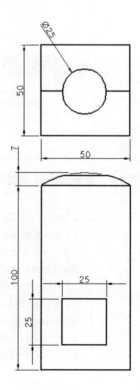

5. Figure 10.40 shows a rendering of a cover for a smoke alarm box. A front view of the cover is shown in Fig. 10.41. There are 12 rectangular slots in the cover. Construct the 3D model of the cover to the sizes given in Fig. 10.41 and render your model when it is completed.

Fig. 10.40 Exercise 5

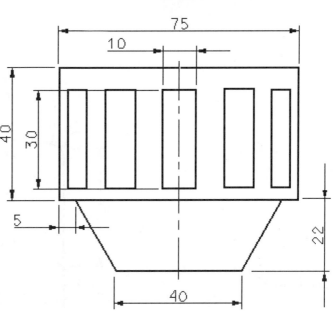

Fig. 10.41 Exercise 5.
Dimensions

6. Figure 10.42 is a rendering of a 3D model of a lamp shade in which 6 holes of 16 mm diameter have been cut. Figure 10.43 shows the dimensions of the Smart Line outline from which the surface of rotation was developed. Construct and render the model.

Fig. 10.42 Exercise 6

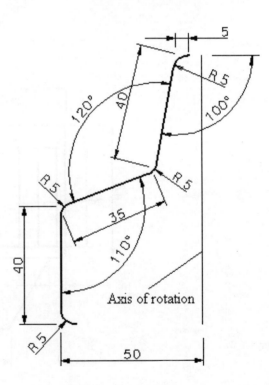

Fig. 10.43 Exercise 6.
Dimensions

CHAPTER 11

The Fillet Surfaces toolbox

Fig. 11.1 The **Fillet Surfaces** flyout

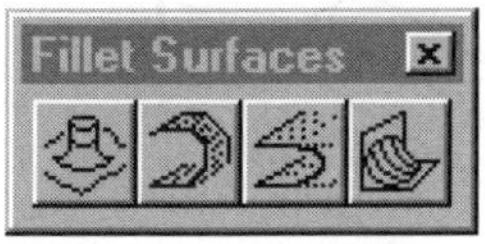

Fig. 11.2 The **Fillet Surfaces** toolbox

Fig. 11.3 The names of the tools in the **Fillet Surfaces** toolbox

Introduction

The four tools in this toolbox can only be effectively used to create fillets, chamfers or blends between surfaces such as cones, surfaces of projection, surfaces of revolution or surfaces constructed with the **Construct Surface by Section** or **Construct Skin Surface** tools.

Holding a *left-click* on the **Construct Fillet Between Surfaces** tool icon brings the toolbox flyout on screen (Fig. 11.1). *Drag* the flyout onto screen and the **Fillet Surfaces** toolbox can be seen (Fig. 11.2). The names of the tools in the toolbox are shown in Fig. 11.3.

Examples of the results of using the tools will be given in a number of examples that follow.

	Construct Fillet Between Surfaces
	Construct Chamfer Between Surfaces
	Blend Surface
	Blend Surface Between Rail Curves

The Construct Fillet Between Surfaces tool

It is important to determine the required direction of the surface normals when constructing a fillet between surfaces. If they are pointing in the wrong direction the tool will not produce fillets between surfaces. To check the direction of the normals to a surface use the **Change Surface Normal** tool in the **Modify 3D Surfaces** toolbox. The use of this tool was shown in Chapter 5.

First example (Fig. 11.4)

1. Construct four surfaces to form a rectangular tube from Smart Lines with the aid of the **Construct Surface by Section** tool. Figure 11.5 shows the tube made up from the four surfaces.

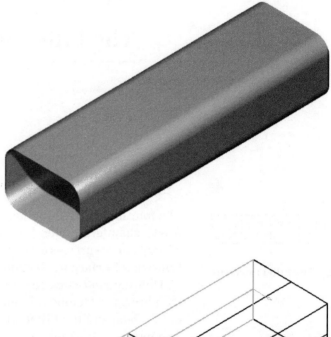

Fig. 11.4 A rendering of the first example

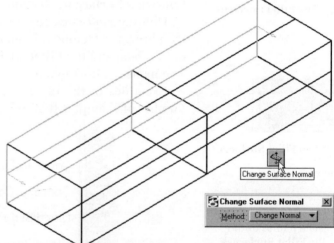

Fig. 11.5 Surface normals must be pointing inwards to create a fillet

2. Call the **Change Surface Normal** tool and *left-click* on surface. If the normals do not point inwards as shown in both Fig. 11.5 and Fig. 11.6 *left-click* to change them. When the normals are facing inwards, in the direction in which the fillets are to be formed, a *right-click* will set them in that direction while the **Change Surface Normal** is in action.

3. Call the **Construct Fillet Between Surfaces** tool.

4. In the tool's Element Selection box, set **Define by:** to Constant Radius; **Truncate:** to Both; the **Tolerance** check box on (**X** in the check box) and set to 1; **Radius** set to 5 – depending upon the size of the surfaces.

5. The Status bar prompts are:

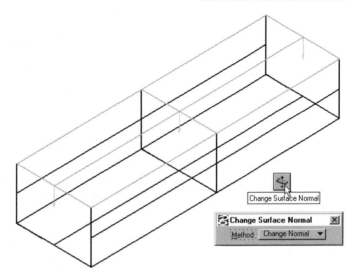

Fig. 11.6 Surface normals must be pointing inwards on both surfaces to be filleted

Construct Fillet Between Surfaces > Identify first surface *pick* one of the surfaces. Its normals are displayed.

Construct Fillet Between Surfaces > Accept/Reject if normals are facing inwards *left-click*.

Construct Fillet Between Surfaces > Identify second surface *pick* the second surface. Its normals are displayed.

Construct Fillet Between Surfaces > Accept/Reject if normals are facing inwards *left-click*. The fillet forms.

Construct Fillet Between Surfaces > Accept/Reject if satisfied with the fillet *left-click*.

Figure 11.7 shows the result of the formation of two of the fillets.

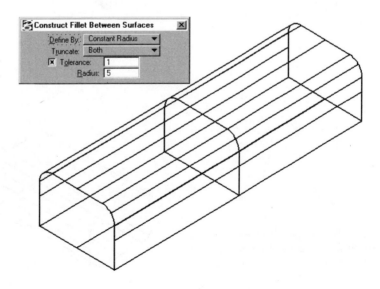

Fig. 11.7 Two of the fillets formed

6. Continue in this manner until all four fillets have been constructed as shown in the rendering of Fig. 11.4.

Second example (Fig. 11.8)

1. Construct another surface from Smart lines at the end of the filleted tube.
2. To construct fillets between the filleted tube and this new surface, the surface normals must be facing outwards – that is in the direction in which the fillet will be formed. Their direction can again be set with the aid of the **Change Surface Normal** tool. Figures 11.8 and 11.9 show the correct direction of the normals for two of the surfaces which are to be filleted.

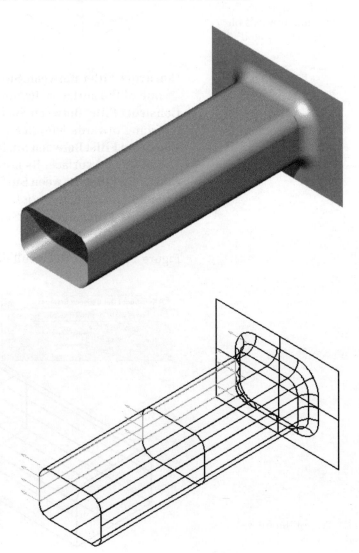

Fig. 11.8 A rendering of the second example

Fig. 11.9 The correct direction of the surface normals for one of the surfaces

3. When satisfied with the direction of the surface normals, fillet between each of the eight surfaces of the tube (the four flat surfaces and the four fillets) as in the procedure given for the first example.

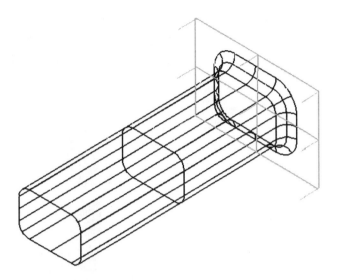

Fig. 11.10 The correct direction of the surface normals for the end surface

Third example (Fig. 11.11)

1. Construct a cone and a surface cylinder to intersect as shown in Fig. 11.11. Depending upon the sizes of the two surfaces, set the parameters in the tool's Element Selection box as for the first example.
2. Following the procedure of creating a fillet already given, add a fillet between the two surfaces.

Fig. 11.11 A rendering of the third example

Fourth example (Fig. 11.12)

In this example a surface of revolution has been constructed to form the outline of a vase. A handle formed from a tubular surface has been added to the vase. The surface between the surface of revolution and the tubular surface has been filleted.

Fig. 11.12 A rendering of the fourth example

Notes

1. It may be necessary to delete lines and arcs from which surfaces have been constructed when fillets have been created between surfaces.
2. If the **Truncate:** option is set to **Both**, then the unwanted parts of the surfaces after filleting has taken place will be automatically trimmed.
3. It is advisable to practise forming fillets with other settings in the tool's Element Selection box in order to acquaint oneself with the possibilities of filleting between surfaces.

The Construct Chamfer Between Surfaces tool

The method of forming a chamfer between surface with the tool is practically identical to the method of forming a fillet previously given.

First example (Fig. 11.13)

1. Construct four surfaces to form a square tube from Smart Lines with the aid of the **Construct Surface by Section** tool. Figure 11.14 shows a rendering of the tube made up from the four surfaces. Ensure that the surface normals of all four surfaces are pointing inwards.

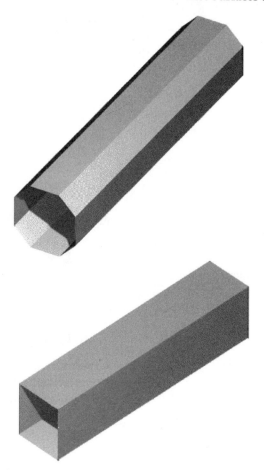

Fig. 11.13 A rendering of the first example

Fig. 11.14 A rendering of the square tube for the first example

2. The Status bar prompts are:

Construct Chamfer Between Surfaces > Identify first surface
pick one of the surfaces. Its normals are displayed.

Construct Chamfer Between Surfaces > Accept/Reject if normals
are facing inwards *left-click*.

Construct Chamfer Between Surfaces > Identify second surface
pick the second surface. Its normals are displayed.

Construct Chamfer Between Surfaces > Accept/Reject if normals
are facing inwards *left-click*. The fillet forms.

Construct Chamfer Between Surfaces > Accept/Reject if satisfied
with the fillet *left-click*.

Second example (Fig. 11.15)

In this example a rectangular tube constructed from a block and a
circle which have been acted upon by the **Construct Surface of**

Projection tool have been placed so as to intersect each other. The surface between the two projections has then been chamfered with the aid of the **Construct Chamfer Between Surfaces** tool.

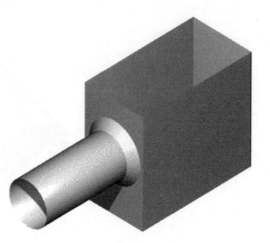

Fig. 11.15 A rendering of the second example

Fillets and chamfers between other surfaces

The examples which follow are based upon two surfaces, one formed from two arcs, the other from two Smart Lines, both with the aid of the **Construct Surface by Section** tool (Fig. 11.16).

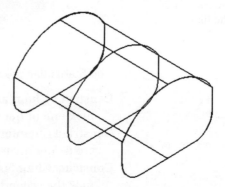

Fig. 11.16 The two surfaces for the examples which follow

First example – fillets between surfaces (Fig. 11.17)

Construct the two surfaces, then call the **Construct Fillet Between Surfaces** tool. Select each surface in turn. Make sure the surface normals are pointing inwards and form the fillet.

Second example – chamfers between surfaces (Fig. 11.18)

This example shows that chamfers between two surfaces can be formed equally as well as can fillets. Again the surface normals must

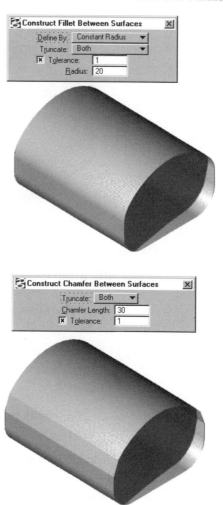

Fig. 11.17 First example – fillets between the two surfaces

Fig. 11.18 Second example – chamfers between the two surfaces

be facing inwards for the chamfers to form. That is they must be facing in the direction in which the chamfering is to take place.

Third example – blending the two surfaces (Fig. 11.19)

1. Call the **Blend Surfaces** tool. In the tool's Element Selection box make settings as shown in Fig. 11.19.
2. The Status bar prompts show:

   Blend Surfaces > Identify first surface at blend point *pick* an edge of one of the surfaces.

   Blend Surfaces > Accept at edge to blend *left-click* if the ghosting is acceptable.

   Blend Surfaces > Identify second surface at blend point *pick* an edge of the second surface.

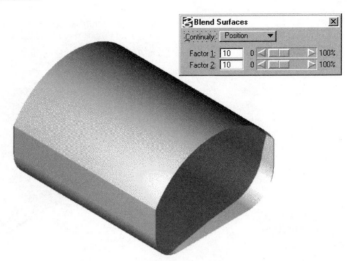

Fig. 11.19 Third example.
Blending the two surfaces

Blend Surfaces > Accept at edge to blend *pick* the proposed blend
    edge at required point.
Blend Surfaces > Accept/Reject *left-click* if the ghosted result is
    as required.

The two surfaces have now been blended and can be acted upon as
a single surface. The fourth example proves that a single surface has
been formed.

**Fourth example – trimming the blended surface (Fig.
11.20)**

1. Add another plane as shown in Fig. 11.21 formed from two Smart
    Lines with **Construct Surface by Section**.
2. Call the **Trim Surfaces** tool and trim both surfaces. The result is as
    shown in Fig. 11.20. If the blended surfaces were not a single
    surface the trimming would not occur as shown in the resulting
    rendered illustration.

Fig. 11.20 Fourth example.
Trimming a blended surface.
A rendering of the result

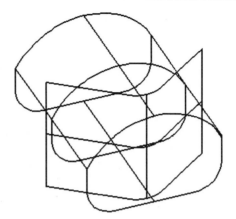

Fig. 11.21 Fourth example.
Adding another surface

Exercises

1. Figure 11.22 is an end view of a section of two meeting half round gutters joined by a down pipe. Figure 11.23 is a rendering of the three surfaces after trimming of the parts.

    Construct the three surfaces and complete the trimming between the parts. Hint – it may be necessary to add a flat surface between the two gutter sections at an angle of 45° to each to obtain a good trim between the two gutters.

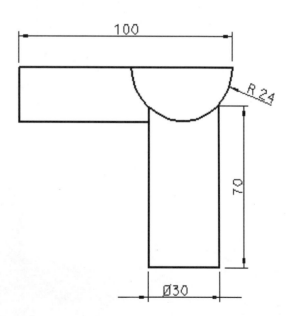

Fig. 11.22 Exercise 1. Sizes

2. Figure 11.24 shows the sizes for the three parts of this exercise. A pipe of 220 mm diameter meets a section of a corrugated roof surface. The roof surface was formed from arcs with the aid of the **Construct Surface by Section** tool.

Fig. 11.23 Exercise 1

Construct the two surfaces and fillet them at a radius of 25 mm. The resulting filleted surfaces are shown in a rendering Fig. 11.25.

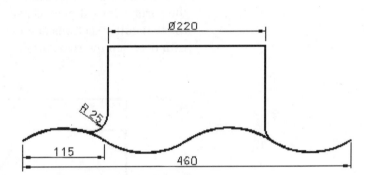

Fig. 11.24 Exercise 2. Sizes

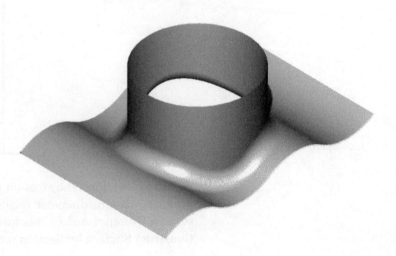

Fig. 11.25 Exercise 2

3. Figure 11.26 gives the dimensions to which the part of this exercise should be drawn. Figure 11.27 is a rendering of the completed 3D model for the exercise.

Working to the given dimensions construct the 3D model.

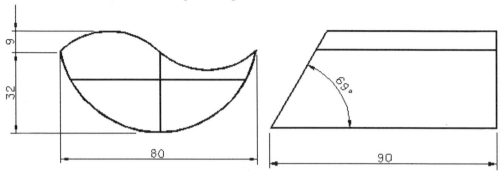

Fig. 11.26 Exercise 3. Sizes

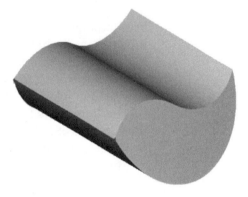

Fig. 11.27 Exercise 3

4. Figure 11.28 is a smooth rendering of a junction box. The box is a 100 mm cube without a top. The pipes are 50 mm diameter and 50 mm long and the fillets are of a radius of 10 mm.

Construct the junction box to these dimensions and if desired render the resulting 3D model.

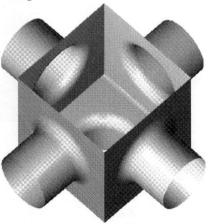

Fig. 11.28 Exercise 4

CHAPTER 12

MicroStation Modeler

Introduction

MicroStation Modeler is an add-on software package which works within MicroStation. Modeler software is for the creating of 3D models and has a number of tools distinct from the 3D tools available in MicroStation 95. The version of Modeler used to produce the illustrations in this and the next chapters was the version shown in Fig. 12.1. The information shown in Fig. 12.1 was brought onto screen by selecting **About MicroStation Modeler** from the **Help** pull-down menu when in MicroStation 95.

The software is loaded into the same directory system as are the files for MicroStation 95, and once loaded, the Modeler tools work seamlessly within MicroStation.

MicroStation Modeler deserves a book in its own right and in order to introduce the use of the software in this book only a

Fig. 12.1 About MicroStation Modeler

selective range of the Modeler tools will be described in this and the following chapter in a series of examples.

The toolboxes in Modeler

Select **Modeler** from the **Tools** pull down-menu (Fig. 12.2). All the toolboxes available in the software will be seen in the sub-menu which appears. Call the **Modeler** toolbox onto screen and replace the **3D Tools** toolbox with the **Modeler** toolbox (Fig. 12.3).

From each tool icon in the toolbox, *drag* out the flyouts to bring all toolboxes on screen. Figure 12.4 shows all the toolboxes *dragged* from the **Modeler** toolbox.

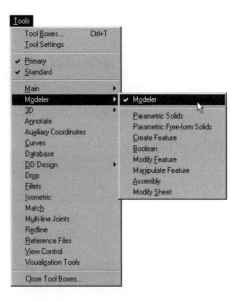

Fig. 12.2 Select **Modeler** from the **Tools** pull-down menu

Notes

1. Some of the tools in the **Modeler** toolboxes will have similar names to those in the **3D Tools** toolboxes. However the results of their use can only be effective when constructing 3D models with other **Modeler** tools. Some solids produced with tools from the **3D Tools** toolboxes cannot be used within 3D models constructed with the **Modeler** tools.

2. When constructing 3D models with **Modeler**, outlines from which the models will be created are drawn with MicroStation 95 tools.

3. If an operator is conversant with using MicroStation, he/she should have no difficulty in getting accustomed to creating 3D models with Modeler. The basic methods of construction are the same, including, in particular, the use of AccuDraw.

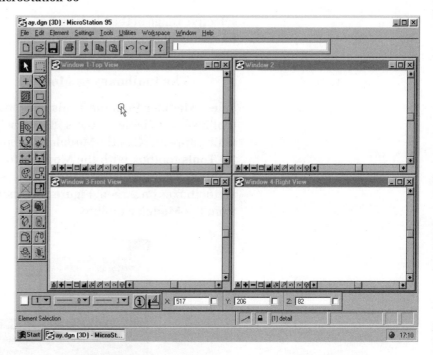

Fig. 12.3 The MicroStation
screen with the **Modeler**
toolbox replacing the **3D Tools**
toolbox

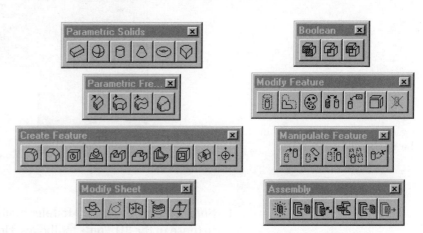

Fig. 12.4 All the toolboxes
from the **Modeler** toolbox

3D models constructed with Modeler tools

First example (Fig. 12.9)

1. Figure 12.5. Construct the given outline with the aid of Smart Line.
2. Figure 12.6. Select the **Construct Projection** tool. Make settings in the tool's Element Selection box as shown and *pick* the outline.
3. Figure 12.7. Select the **Chamfer Edge** tool. Make settings in the tool's Element Selection box as shown. Work in the **Isometric View** window. The Status bar prompt shows:

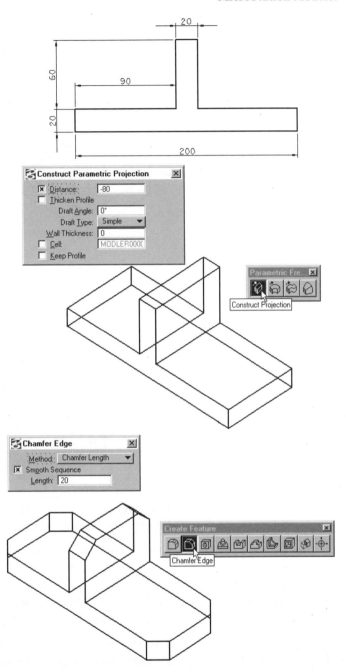

Fig. 12.5 First example.
Stage 1

Fig. 12.6 First example.
Stage 2

Fig. 12.7 First example.
Stage 3

Chamfer Edge > Identify edge *Pick* one of the edges to be
chamfered. That edge highlights and the prompt changes to
Chamfer Edge > Identify next edge or RESET to reject *Pick* each
of the other three edges in turn. They highlight as *picked*.
When all four edges have been *picked*, *right-click* and the
edges chamfer.

4. Figure 12.8. Select the **Create Hole** tool. Make settings in the tool's Element Selection box as shown. Working in the **Isometric View**

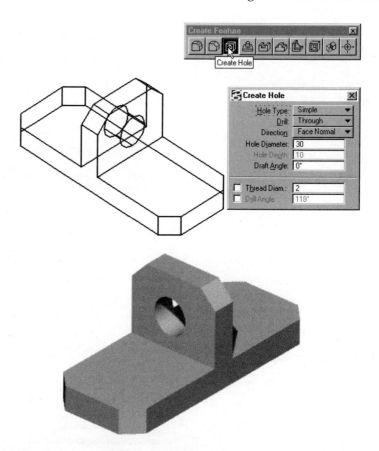

Fig. 12.8 First example.
Stage 4

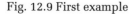

Fig. 12.9 First example

window with the AccuDraw compass in its **Side** position (press the **S** key). The Status bar prompt becomes:

Create Hole > Identify solid *pick* the solid. A ghosted hole appears centred at the cursor hair line intersection. *Drag* the hole into position as required.

Create Hole > Accept/Reject if satisfied *left-click* to accept. The hole forms. *Right-click.*

5. The 3D model is now completed. If desired it can be rendered. Figure 12.9 shows a **Phong Antialias** rendering of the first example.

Second example (Fig. 12.14)

1. Figure 12.10. In the **Front View** window construct the outline with the aid of Smart Line as shown.

2. Figure 12.11. With the **Construct Projection** tool, create a projection 80 mm deep from the outline.

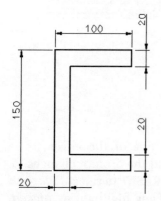

Fig. 12.10 Second example.
Stage 1

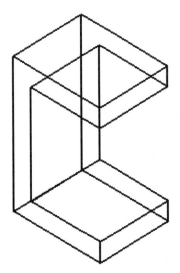

Fig. 12.11 Example 2. Stage 2

3. Figure 12.12. Select the **Rounded Edge or Vertex** tool. Make setting in the tool's Element Selection box as shown. The Status bar prompt shows:

Round Edge > Identify edge *pick* one of the edges to be rounded. It highlights.

Round Edge > Identify next edge or RESET to finish *pick* each of the other edges in turn. They highlight as *picked*. *Right-click* and all edges become rounded.

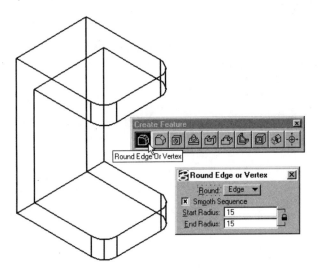

Fig. 12.12 Second example. Stage 3

4. Figure 12.13. Select the **Construct Circular Boss** tool. Make settings in the tool's Element Selection box as shown. Work in the **Isometric View** window. Set the AccuDraw compass to its **Top** view (**T** key).

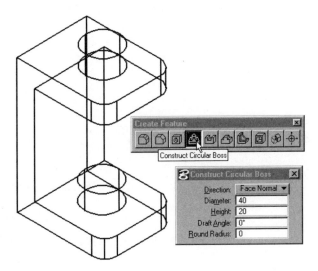

Fig. 12.13 Second example. Stage 4

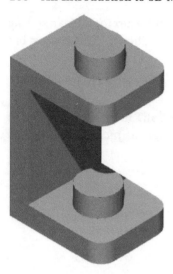

Fig. 12.14 Second example

The Status bar shows:

Construct Circular Boss > Identify solid *pick* the solid.

Construct Circular Boss > Accept/Reject a boss appears at the cursor intersections ready to be *dragged* into position. *Pick* its position and *left-click*. The other boss position can then be *picked* followed by a *left-click*. When completed *right-click*.

5. Figure 12.14. The 3D model can be rendered if thought desirable. A **Phong Antialias** rendering is shown.

Third example (Fig. 12.16)

1. Figure 12.15. Construct the outline as shown working to any convenient sizes.
2. Figure 12.15. Select the **Construct Revolution** tool. Make settings in the tool's Element Selection box as shown. Work in the **Isometric View** window. Set the AccuDraw compass to its **Top** view (**T** key). The Status bar shows:

Construct Parametric Revolution > Identify profile *pick* the outline.

Construct Parametric Revolution > Define radius *left-click* (radius already defined in Element Selection box). The solid of revolution forms.

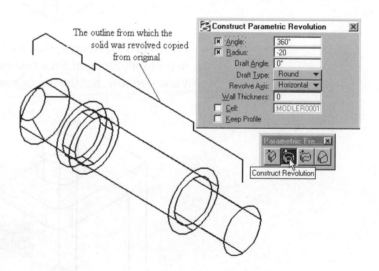

Fig. 12.15 Third example.
Stages 1 and 2

3. Figure 12.16. Render the 3D model if desired.

Fourth example (Fig. 12.21)

1. Figure 12.17. In the **Front View** window, construct the outline as shown.

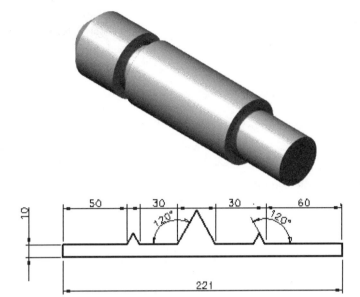

Fig. 12.16 Third example

Fig. 12.17 Fourth example.
Stage 1

2. Figure 12.18. Create a parametric projection from the outline in the **Isometric View** window as shown.

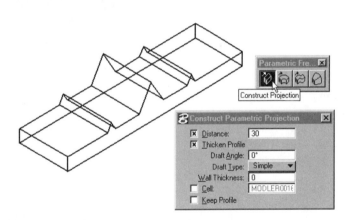

Fig. 12.18 Fourth example.
Stage 2.

3. Figure 12.19. Still working in the **Isometric View** window, and using the **Round Edge or Vertex** tool, with settings as shown, form the ends of the solid into semicircular shape.
4. Figure 12.20. Still using the **Round Edge or Vertex** tool form rounded edges of radius of either 3 mm or 5 mm at the angles in the 3D model.
5. Figure 12.20. With the **Create Hole** tool and with the aid of the **Center** snap, create holes as shown working to the settings as given in Fig. 12.20 in the tool's Element Selection box.
6. Figure 12.21. Render the 3D model if desired.

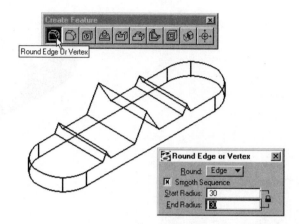

Fig. 12.19 Fourth example.
Stage 3

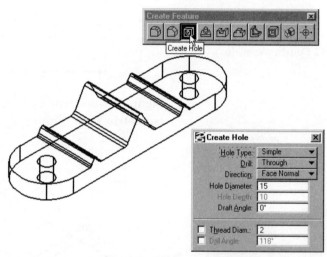

Fig. 12.20 Fourth example.
Stages 4 and 5

Fig. 12.21 Fourth example

Fifth example (Fig. 12.26)

1. Figure 12.22. Construct the outline as shown in the **Front View** window.

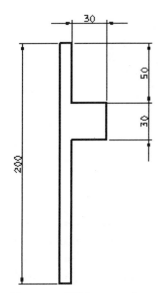

Fig. 12.22 Fifth example.
Stage 1

Fig. 12.23 Fifth example.
Stage 2

Fig. 12.24 Fifth example.
Stage 3

2. Figure 12.23. Form a surface of projection from the outline and with **Construct Projection** tool form a solid of length 200 mm. In the solid, with the **Round Edge or Vertex** tool round the lower front edge 15 mm and the upper two edges of the back 20 mm. Then with the **Create Hole** tool and with the aid of the **Center** snap, create a hole of diameter 20 mm through the solid.

3. Figure 12.24. Construct two wedges as shown. Make the wedges larger than necessary and deeper than required – say even 10 mm deep.

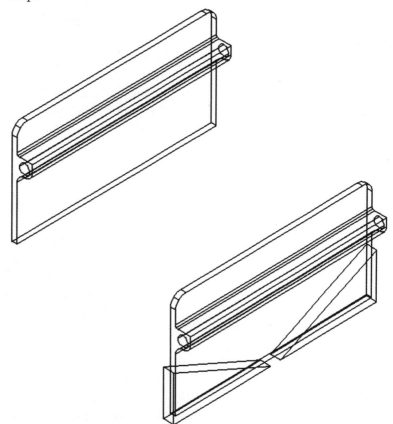

4. Figure 12.25. Select the Boolean operator **Construct Solids Difference**. The Status bar will show:

Construct Solids Difference > Identify solid *pick* the main body of the model.
Construct Solids Difference > Accept/Reject (select next input) *pick* each of the wedges in turn.
Construct Solids Difference > Accept/Reject (select next input) *left-click* and the difference is created.

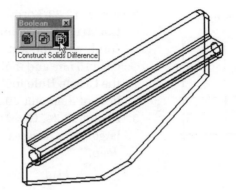

Fig. 12.25 Fifth example.
Stage 4

5. Figure 12.26. Use **Round Edge or Vertex** to fillet all four corners at the bottom. Add 20 mm diameter holes at the centre point of each of the rounded corners. The model can now be rendered. Figure 12.26 shows an addition to the top of the protruding part, which can be added if desired.

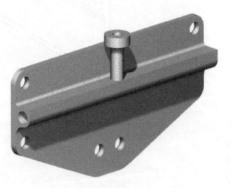

Fig. 12.26 Fifth example

Notes:

1. It may be necessary to use the MicroStation 95 **Move** tool to position some features when constructing a 3D model consisting of several parts. The moving may have to be performed in several windows – **Top**, **Front** and **Right**. However, providing good use is made of the AccuDraw compass and the snaps from the Button bar, it is possibly best to work in the **Isometric View** window.

Exercises

1. Figures 12.27 and 12.28 show the dimensions for, and the rendered view of, a handle fixed to a bar and pin. Construct the model using Modeler tools.

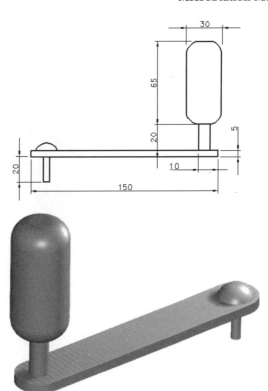

Fig. 12.27 Exercise 1.
Dimensions

Fig. 12.28 Exercise 1

2. Figures 12.29 and 12.30 show the dimensions and a rendering of the 3D model for this exercise. Using tools from the Modeler toolboxes, construct the model. Use the Boolean operator **Construct Solids Union** to join the three parts of the model.

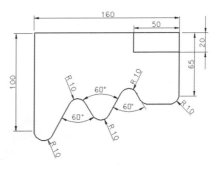

Fig. 12.29 Exercise 2.
Dimensions

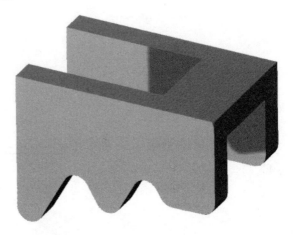

Fig. 12.30 Exercise 2

3. Figures 12.31 and 12.32 show the dimensions and a rendering of the 3D model for this exercise. Use **Construct Solids Union** to join the parts of the model.

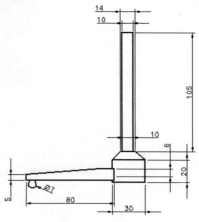

Fig. 12.31 Exercise 3.
Dimensions

Fig. 12.32 Exercise 3

CHAPTER 13

More Modeler examples

Introduction

The examples of 3D models constructed with the aid of Modeler tools given in this chapter are somewhat more complex than those shown in Chapter 12, but still involve a limited range of the Modeler tools. When working with Modeler tools, the method of working can usually follow the procedure:

1. Construct outlines in **Top**, **Front** or **Right** view windows, using tools such as **Smart Line**, **Place Circle**, **Place Arc** and making full use of the Button bar snaps.
2. Where necessary use the tools from the **Group** toolbox to ensure outlines can be projected into solids of various forms.
3. Construct the 3D models from the outlines working mainly in the **Isometric View** window and making full use of the various placements possible with the AccuDraw compass, in particular the keyboard shortcuts – **T** for **Top View** position; **F** for **Front View** position; **S** for **Right View** position.
4. While constructing the 3D models in the **Isometric View** window, make full use of the **Snap Mode** snaps – **Keypoint**, **Midpoint**, **Center** etc. from the Button bar.

First example (Fig. 13.1)

1. Working to the dimensions given in Fig. 13.2 and with the aid of **Smart Line** and **Circle** construct the outline of the back in the **Front View** window and of the top piece in the **Top View** window. Form each of the outlines into groups with the aid of the **Group Hole** tool.
2. Figure 13.3. With **Construct Projection** project the two outlines into solids of projection each 20 mm high. With **Copy** copy the top piece to provide the bottom piece.
4. Figure 13.4. Using the **Midpoint** snap from the Button bar, move the upper and lower parts into their correct position while in the **Isometric View** window.

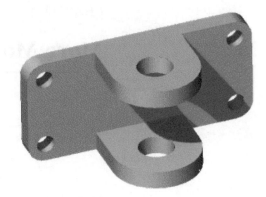

Fig. 13.1 First example

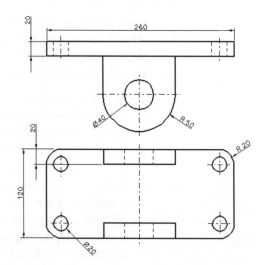

Fig. 13.2 First example
Dimensions

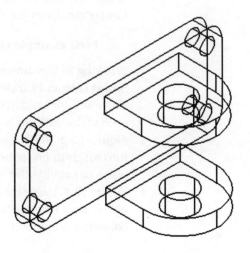

Fig. 13.3 First example.
Stage 3

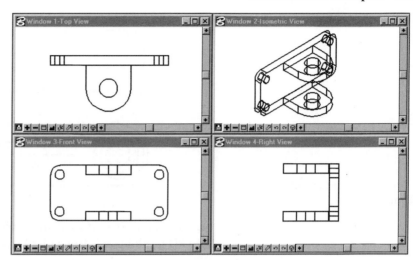

Fig. 13.4 First example.
Stage 4

5. Figure 13.5. With the **Construct Solids Union** tool form the three projections into a single solid.
6. Render the model if thought desirable as shown in Fig. 13.1.

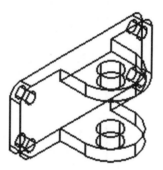

Fig. 13.5 First example.
Stage 5

Second example (Fig. 13.6)

1. Working to the dimensions given in Fig. 13.7, construct an outline for the base of the model in the **Top View** window. Create a group form the outlines

Fig. 13.6 Second example

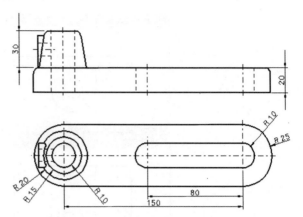

Fig. 13.7 Second example.
Dimensions

2. Figure 13.8. With the **Construct Projection** tool, change the outlines into 3D model projections of 20 mm height.

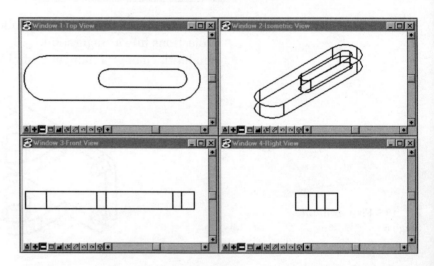

Fig. 13.8 Second example.
Stage 2

3. Figure 13.9. With the **Round Edge or Vertex** tool fillet the edges of the base at 5 mm radius.

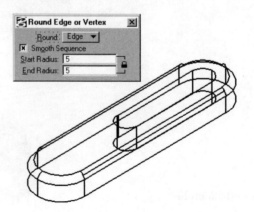

Fig. 13.9 Second example.
Stage 3

4. Figure 13.10. Construct an outline for a surface of revolution for the boss and with the aid of the **Construct Revolution** create the boss.

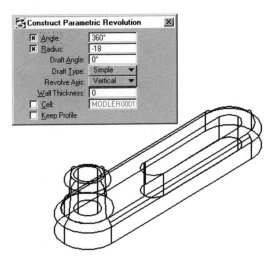

Fig. 13.10 Second example. Stage 4

5. Figure 13.11. Construct an outline in the **Right View** window for the flange to the boss and with **Construct Projection** project it to a height of 5 mm. Then if the parts of the model require to be moved to their final positions, use **Move** with AccuDraw to do so. Then with **Construct Solids Union** form a union of the three parts.

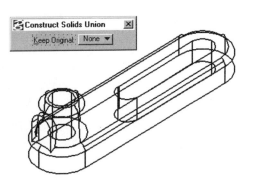

Fig. 13.11 Second example. Stage 5

6. Figure 13.12. With the **Create Hole** tool form the hole in the flange and boss, using the **Center** snap to place the hole in its correct position.
7. The model can now be rendered if thought desirable as in Fig. 13.6.

Third example (Fig. 13.13)

This third example is adding a tool rest to the model of a tool holder constructed in the second example. The model was constructed with the aid of the **Construct Projection**, **Construct Revolution**,

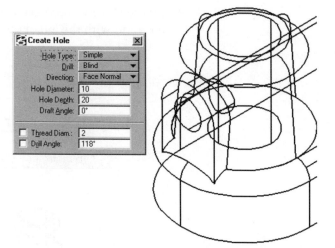

Fig. 13.12 Second example.
Stage 6

Round Edge or Vertex, **Construct Solids Union** and **Construct Solids Difference** tools. Figure 13.14 shows the last stage in the construction of this example.

Fig. 13.13 Third example

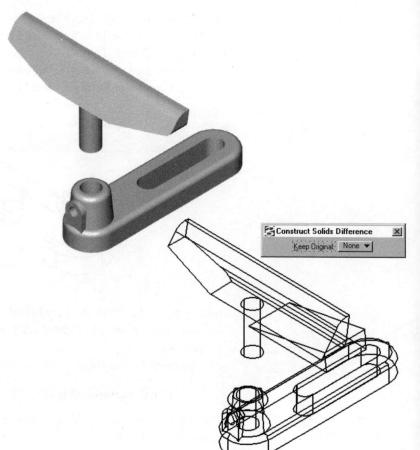

Fig. 13.14 The final stage in the construction of the third example

Fourth example (Fig. 13.15)

This example is a further addition to the third example by adding a tightening screw. It will be noted in this example that the screw thread has not been included as being too advanced for this example in this introductory book.

Fig. 13.15 Fourth example

Figure 13.16 shows the tightening screw without its thread in an enlarged detail view taken from the **Isometric View** window. A rendering of the example is given in Fig. 13.15. The screw was constructed in several parts from revolved surfaces derived from outlines. The various parts were then united with the aid of the **Construct Solids Union** tool.

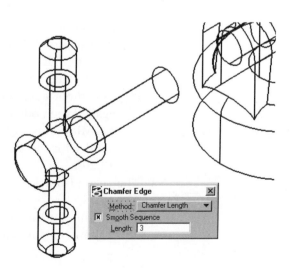

Fig. 13.16 An enlarged view of the tightening screw from the fourth example

Fifth example (Fig. 13.17)

This is a 3D model of a bathroom fitting constructed in Modeler. It consists of three parts – two brackets which hold the third part – a rail with rounded edges. Details of the dimensions of the fitment are given in Fig. 13.18.

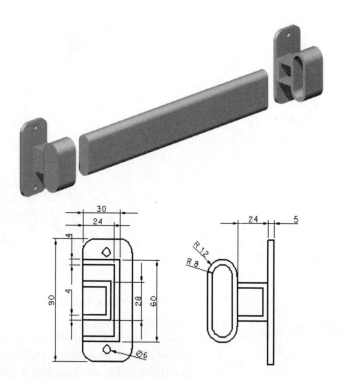

Fig. 13.17 Fifth example

Fig. 13.18 Fifth example. Dimensions

1. A single bracket was constructed as follows:
   (a) The element with rounded ends was made up from two projections one inside the other. They were then acted upon by the **Construct Solids Difference** tool to form hollow rounded end box. The open ended boxlike element was made up in a similar manner.
   (b) The three elements (Fig. 13.19) were moved to fit tightly against each other – **Move** tool plus the use of AccuDraw and the **Midpoint** snap. They were then joined together as a single solid with the side of the **Construct Solids Union** tool (Fig. 13.20).
2. The second bracket was formed by using the **Mirror** tool (Fig. 13.21).
3. The outline for the end of the rail was then constructed. Figure 13.22 shows the four view windows MicroStation 95 screen at this stage.

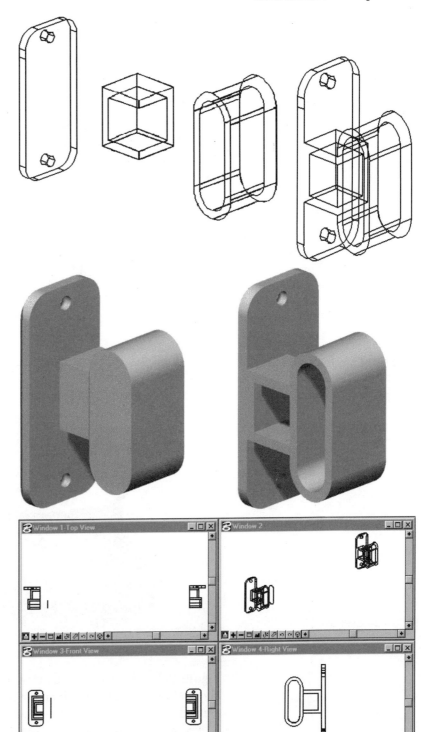

Fig. 13.19 Fifth example. Stage 1

Fig. 13.20 Fifth example. Result of Stage 1

Fig. 13.21 Fifth example. Stage 2

Fig. 13.22 Fifth example. Stage 3. The four view windows

4. The rails was constructed from its outline with **Construct Projection** to a length of 300 mm.

5. The 3D model could then be rendered as shown in Fig. 13.17.

Exercises

1. Figure 13.23 is a front view and a plan in third angle projection of a part from a gear box. A rendering of the part is given in Fig. 13.24. Working to the dimensions given construct a 3D model of the part. Dimensions not given can be estimated.

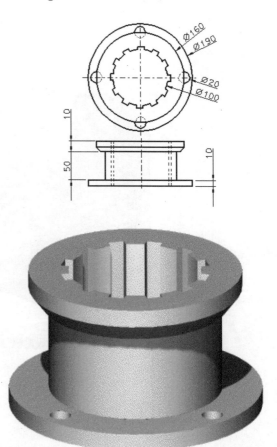

Fig. 13.23 Exercise 1. Dimensions

Fig. 13.24 Exercise 1

2. Figure 13.25 is a cross section through the rim of the pulley wheel shown in Fig. 13.26. The diameter of the pulley is 400 mm and its central hole is 80 mm in diameter.

From the dimensions given in Fig. 13.25 and working to the diameters given above, construct a 3D model of the pulley.

Figure 13.26 is a rendering of the completed pulley.

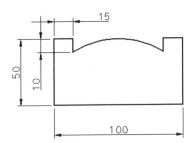

Fig. 13.25 Exercise 2.
Dimensions of rim of pulley

Fig. 13.26 Exercise 2

3. Figure 13.27 gives the dimensions in a front view of the bracket shown in a rendering in Fig. 13.28. The bracket is 80 mm deep from front to back.

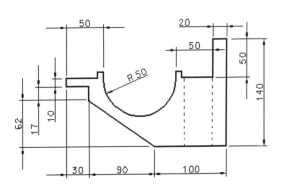

Fig. 13.27 Exercise 3.
Dimensions

Construct a 3D model of the bracket and render as shown in Fig. 13.28.

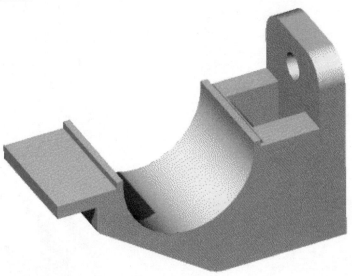

Fig. 13.28 Exercise 3

4. Figure 13.29 is a front view and plan in third angle projection of an engineering component. Working to the given dimensions construct a 3D model of the component.

When completed render your model as shown in Fig. 13.30.

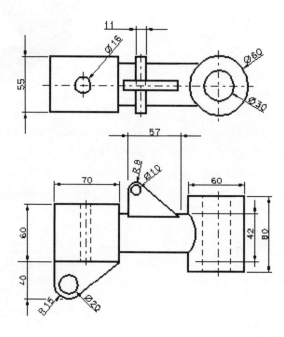

Fig. 13.29 Exercise 4.
Dimensions

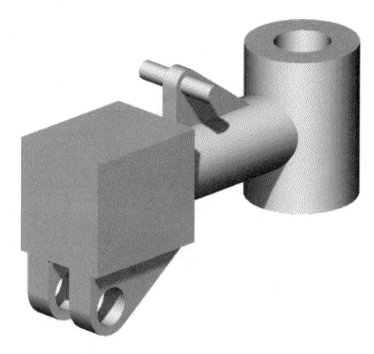

Fig. 13.30 Exercise 4

5. A third angle projection of one end of a coupling is given in Fig. 13.31. A rendering of the completed 3D model is given in Fig. 13.32.

Working to the dimensions given with Fig. 13.31. Construct one part of the coupling. Then mirror your model to gain the other end. The pins and coupling stud can then be added. The resulting 3D model is shown in Fig. 13.32.

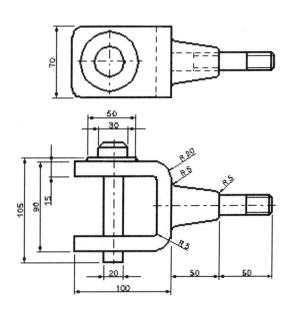

Fig. 13.31 Exercise 5.
Dimensions

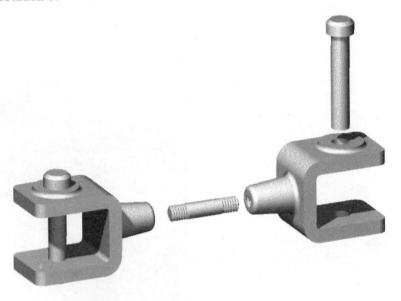

Fig. 13.32 Exercise 5

CHAPTER 14

Other Modeler tools

Introduction

In this chapter, examples of simple 3D models constructed with the aid of the following tools from the MicroStation Modeler toolboxes will be shown:

> From the **Parametric Free-form Solids** toolbox – **Construct Tubular Solid** and **Construct Skinned Solid**.
> From the **Create Feature** toolbox – **Construct Rib, Construct Thin Skinned Solid** and **Create Solid Section**.
> From the **Modify Feature** toolbox – **Modify Solid or Feature, Modify Profile, Annotate Feature** and **Drop Solid to Components**.

Although these other Modeler tools do not include examples in this introductory book of all the Modeler tools, sufficient have been included to introduce the reader to the possibilities of constructing 3D models with the aid of the software.

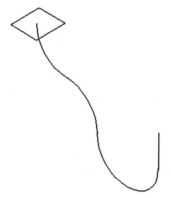

Fig. 14.1 **Construct Tubular Solid**. First example. Trace curve and section profile

The Construct Tubular Solid tool

First example (Fig. 14.2)

1. In the **Front View** window construct a trace curve for the tube and in the **Top View** window construct a section profile (Fig. 14.1).
2. In the **Parametric Free-form Solids** toolbox, *left-click* on the icon of the **Construct Tubular Solid** tool. The Status bar shows the prompt:

Construct Parametric Tubular Solid > Identify trace curve *pick* the trace curve.

Construct Parametric Tubular Solid > Identify section profile *pick* the profile.

Construct Parametric Tubular Solid > Accept/Reject *left-click* and the tubular solid forms (Fig. 14.2).

Fig. 14.2 **Construct Tubular Solid**. First example

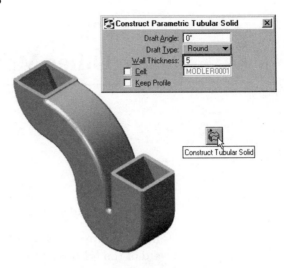

Second example (Fig. 14.4)

In this example the trace curve is a Smart line set with chamfers and the Section profile a circle (Fig. 14.3). The resulting tubular surface is shown in Fig. 14.4.

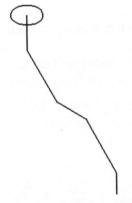

Fig. 14.3 **Construct Tubular Solid**. Second example. Trace curve and section profile

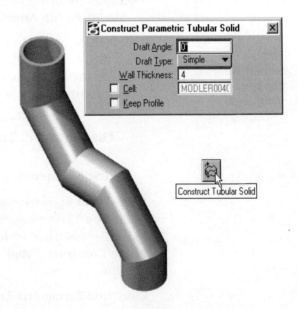

Fig. 14.4 **Construct Tubular Solid**. Second example

The Construct Skinned Solid tool

The results of using this tool are similar to those resulting from the use of the **Construct Surface by Section** tool from the **3D Tools** toolbox (page 44).

First example (Fig. 14.6)

1. Construct a series of section profiles (Fig. 14.5).

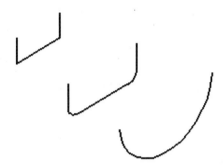

Fig. 14.5 **Construct Skinned
Solid**. First example. The
section outlines

2. Select the **Construct Skinned Solid** tool. The Status bar prompt
   shows:

   Construct Parametric Skinned Solid > Identify section profile
   pick the first of the profiles.
   **Construct Parametric Skinned Solid > Accept/Reject (select next
   input)** *pick* the next profile.
   **Construct Parametric Skinned Solid > Accept/Reject (select next
   input)** *pick* the next profile.
   **Construct Parametric Skinned Solid > Accept/Reject (select next
   input)** *pick* the next profile.
   **Construct Parametric Skinned Solid > Accept/Reject (select next
   input)** *pick* the next profile *left-click* to accept if satisfied with
   the result. The skinned surface forms in ghosted form.
   **Construct Parametric Skinned Solid > Accept/Reject (select next
   input)** *left-click* if satisfied and the surface is created (Fig.
   14.6).

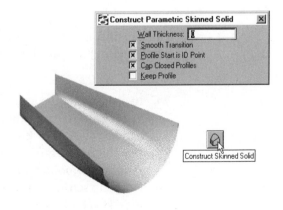

Fig. 14.6 **Construct Skinned
Solid**. First example

Second example (Fig. 14.7)

In this example arcs were used as section profiles and the settings in the tool's Element Selection box were changed as shown in Fig. 14.5. The resulting skinned solid has a surface which is 10 mm thick.

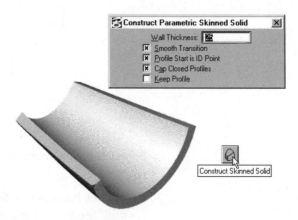

Fig. 14.7 **Construct Skinned Solid**. Second example

The Construct Rib tool

First example (Fig. 14.8)

1. Construct the solid on which the rib is to be added.
2. Select the **Construct Rib** tool from the **Create Feature** toolbox. The Status bar prompt becomes:

   Construct Rib > Identify solid *pick* the solid.
   Construct Rib > Enter rib diagonal endpoint 1 *pick* the required endpoint as in Fig. 14.8.
   Construct Rib > Enter rib diagonal endpoint 2 *pick* the required endpoint as in Fig. 14.8.
   Construct Rib > Enter point on rib body *pick* the required point as in Fig. 14.8.

The resulting ghosted rib can then be accepted (*left-click*) or rejected (*right-click*) to complete or to start again.

   Notes

1. In order to get the exact required points for the positions on a rib it is advisable to construct lines on the solid onto which snap points can be selected as indicated in Fig. 14.8.
2. Use the AccuDraw key shortcuts (**T**op, **F**ront and **S**ide) to assist in *picking* the points on the rib.
3. Note the settings in the tool's Element Selection box as shown in Figs 14.8 and 14.9.

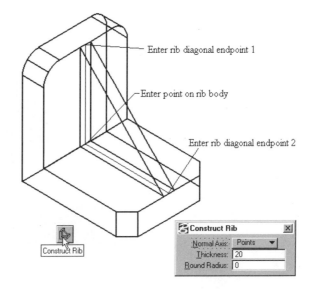

Enter rib diagonal endpoint 1

Enter point on rib body

Enter rib diagonal endpoint 2

Construct Rib

Construct Rib
Normal Axis: Points
Thickness: 20
Round Radius: 0

Fig. 14.8 **Construct Rib**. First example

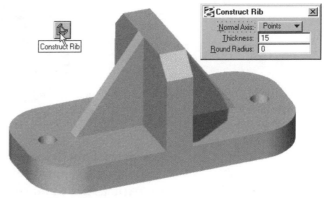

Construct Rib

Construct Rib
Normal Axis: Points
Thickness: 15
Round Radius: 0

Fig. 14.9 **Construct Rib**. Second example

Second example (Fig. 14.9)

This second example shows two ribs formed on a solid.

The Construct Thin Skinned Solid tool

Example (Fig. 14.11)

Figure 14.10 shows a rendering of a simple 3D solid model constructed with the aid of Modeler tools. Figure 14.11 shows the same solid after the action of the **Construct Thin Skinned Solid** tool.

1. Select the tool. The Status bar prompt becomes:

    Construct Thin Skinned Solid > Identify solid *pick* the solid.
    Construct Thin Skinned Solid > Identify face to assign *pick* the upper face of the solid. Its boundary highlights.

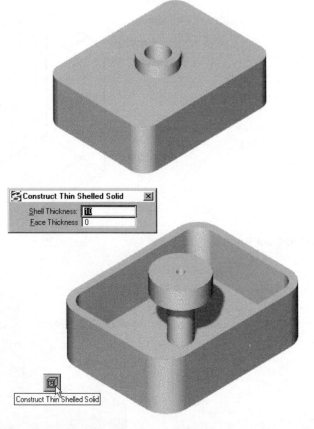

Fig. 14.10 **Construct Thin Skinned Solid**. Example. The original solid

Fig. 14.11 **Construct Thin Skinned Solid**. Example

Construct Thin Skinned Solid > Identify next face or RESET to finish the skinned surface ghosts.

Construct Thin Skinned Solid > Accept thin shell or RESET to finish *left-click* to accept. The result is as in Fig. 14.11.

The Create Solid Section tool

Example (Fig. 14.12)

1. Select the tool.
2. *Pick* points in response to Status bar prompts as indicated in Fig. 14.12.
3. When the section ghosts, *left-click* to accept.

The Modify Solid or Feature tool

Example (Fig. 14.13)

Select the tool from the **Modify Feature** toolbox. The Status bar prompts become:

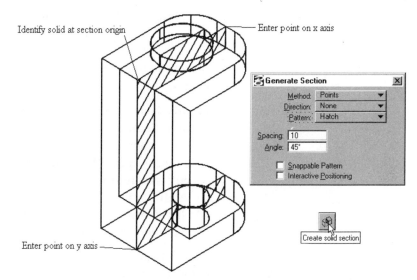

Fig. 14.12 **Create Solid Section**. Example

> **Modify Parametric Solid or Feature > Identify feature** *pick* the feature, which is part of the 3D model.
>
> **Modify Parametric Solid or Feature > Accept/Reject (select next input)** *left-click* again on the feature. The **Edit Projection** dialogue box appears. *Enter* the required modification height in the **Distance:** box and *left-click* on the **OK** button. The feature is modified to the new figure.

In Fig. 14.13, the left-hand drawing shows the original 3D model, the parametric projection of which requires to be modified. The right-hand drawing shows the ghosted feature after *entering* the modification figure.

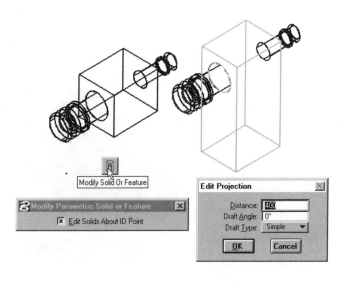

Fig. 14.13 **Modify Solid or Feature**. Example

The Modify Profile tool

Example (Fig. 14.15)

1. Select the tool from the **Modify Feature** toolbox. The Status bar shows:

   Modify Feature > Identify feature *pick* the central projection.

   Modify Feature > Accept/Reject (select next input) *pick* the feature again. The **Modify Profile** dialogue box appears. *Enter* a figure in the **Wall Thickness:** box and *left-click* on the **OK** button of the dialogue box. The feature highlights showing the modification.

   Modify Feature > Accept/Reject (select next input) *left-click* and the selected feature from the 3D model changes as required.

Figure 14.14 shows the feature selected (highlighted), together with the **Modify Profile** dialogue box.

The left-hand rendering of Fig. 14.15 shows the 3D model before modification. The right-hand rendering shows the 3D model with the modified feature.

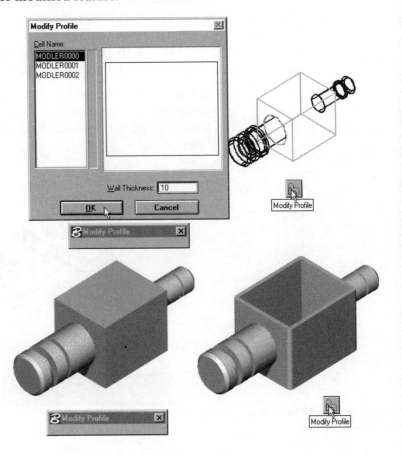

Fig. 14.14 Example. The **Modify Profile** dialogue box

Fig. 14.15 **Modify Profile**. Example

Notes

1. All parts of the 3D model will be shown in the **Cell Name:** list of the dialogue box.
2. The selected feature's name highlights and an outline of the selected feature appears in the pattern box of the dialogue box.

The Annotate Feature tool

Example (Fig. 14.16)

Select the tool from the **Modify Feature** toolbox. The Status bar prompt changes to:

> **Annotate Feature > Identify feature** *pick* the feature – in this example a chamfered end. The **Annotate Feature** dialogue box appears. *Left-click* on the **General Settings** button. The **Chamfer Annotation Settings** box appears. *Enter* suitable annotation in the box. *Left-click* on the chamfer and the annotation appears on screen at the chosen point to be *dragged* to a more suitable position as required.

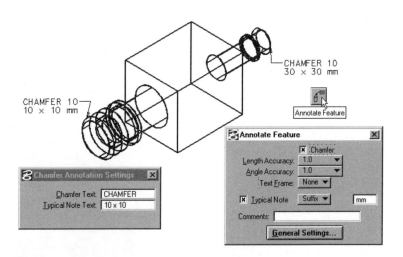

Fig. 14.16 **Annotate Feature**.
Example

The Drop Solid to Components tool

Example (Fig. 14.17)

Select the tool from the **Modify Feature** toolbox and *left-click* on the solid. Now use the **Move** tool to move each face of the solid away from the remainder of the solid.

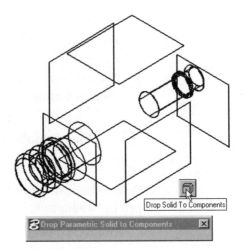

Fig. 14.17 **Drop Solid to Components**. Example

Exercises

The methods of construction of the 3D models is left to the judgement of the reader although the dialogue boxes shown with the illustrations will give some guidance.

1. Figure 14.18 shows a rendering of a 3D model of an air blasting pipe from a forge (a tue). The diameter of the backing piece is 200 mm and it is 25 mm thick. The sizes of the conical tue pipe are given in the dialogue box accompanying Fig. 14.19.

    Construct the 3D model as shown and if thought necessary render your model.

Fig. 14.18 Exercise 1

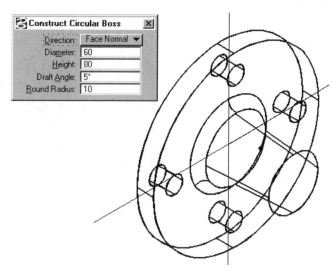

Fig. 14.19 Exercise 1.
Dimensions of the tue

2. Figure 14.20 shows a rendering of a 3D model of a pointing device.
    Some of the dimensions of the model are shown in dialogue boxes
    in Fig. 14.21. A dimensioned two-view orthographic projection of
    the device is given in Fig. 14.22.

    Construct a model of the pointing device. If thought desirable,
    render your completed construction.

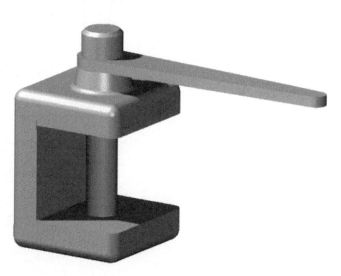

Fig. 14.20 Exercise 2

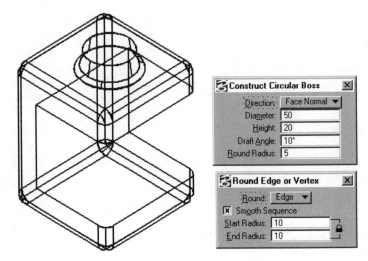

Fig. 14.21 Exercise 2. Some
dimensions in dialogue boxes

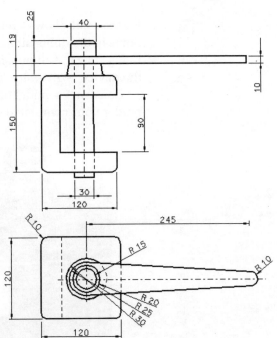

Fig. 14.22 Exercise 2. A two-
view orthographic projection

3. Figure 14.23 shows a rendering of a link from a machine. Figure 14.24 is a two-view orthographic projection of the link. Construct a 3D model of the link to the given sizes.

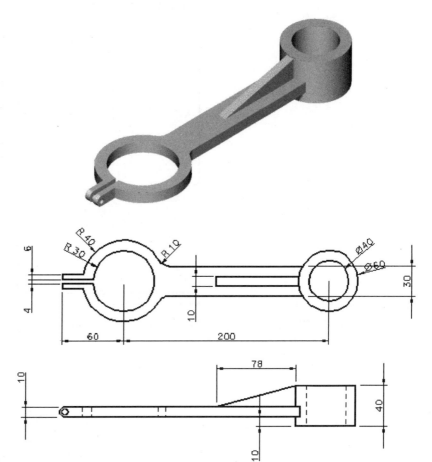

Fig. 14.23 Exercise 3

Fig. 14.24 Exercise 3. A two-view orthographic projection

4. Figure 14.26 is a rendering of a 3D model of a plate from a machine. Figure 14.25 is a three-view orthographic projection of the plate.
   Construct a 3D model to the given dimensions, rendering your model if thought necessary.

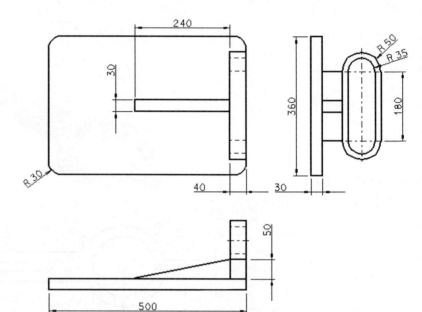

Fig. 14.25 Exercise 4. A three-view orthographic projection

Fig. 14.26 Exercise 4

5. Figure 14.27 shows a rendering of a 3D model of a tank in the form of a cube with edges 225 mm long and with tubes on two sides, that on the left of hexagonal section and that on the right of circular section.

Construct a 3D model to the given dimensions and render your model if you wish.

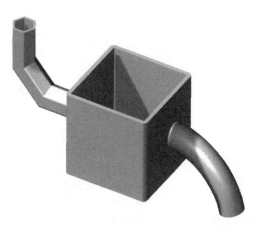

Fig. 14.27 Exercise 5

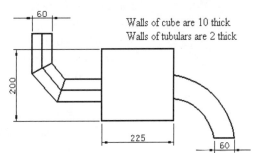

Fig. 14.28 Exercise 5. Some dimensions

CHAPTER 15

Rendering

Introduction

Fig. 15.1 Selecting **Global Lighting** from the **Settings**

A number of the illustrations throughout this book consist of renderings of 3D models which have been constructed in MicroStation 95. Except for the renderings given in the colour plates, they have all been rendered in what is termed greyscale, with all colours from the original scenes on screen in shades of grey. Most of the renderings in the book have been captured from MicroStation 95 screens as screen dumps working to settings made in the **Global Lighting** dialogue box (Fig. 15.2), called to screen by selecting **Rendering** from the **Settings** pull-down menu, followed by selecting **Global Lighting** from the sub-menu which appears (Fig. 15.1). Descriptions of the various settings which can be made in the **Global Lighting** dialogue box will be given in this chapter.

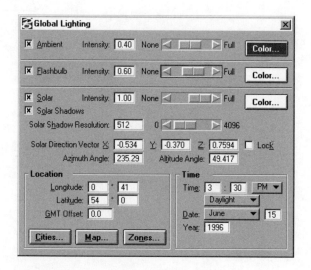

Fig. 15.2 The **Global Lighting** dialogue box showing settings for most of the renderings given in this book

Settings in the Global Lighting dialogue box

Check boxes

Each form of lighting in the dialogue box can be turned off by a *left-click* in the check box against the name of the form of lighting (no **X** in check box). Conversely it can be switched back on again by a *left-click* in an empty check box.

Ambient

Ambient lighting is a general overall lighting of the same intensity anywhere in a scene to be rendered. It has no direction, its intensity being variable from 0 to 1 by adjustment of the **Intensity:** figure – usually by adjusting the slider to the right of the number. A usual setting for Ambient lighting is 0.3 to 0.4. Any higher figure tends to swamp a scene to the detriment of other lighting patterns, lower setting allow features such as shadows to become rather harsh.

Flashbulb

Operates in the same manner as a camera flashbulb given a sharp, overall lighting effect onto the scene from all directions. It is advisable to experiment with flashbulb settings because the effect of this lighting setting can cause too much intensity of a sharp light with harsh shadows.

Solar

The light derived from the sun. A number of controls can be set in connection with solar lighting – **Intensity**, **Shadows**, **Location**, **Day**, **Month** and **Year** as well as the time of the day either a.m. or p.m.

Location

Left-click on the **Cities...** button in the **Location** area and the **Location By City** dialogue box appears (Fig. 15.3) from which a selection can be made from a scrollable list.

Map

Left-click on the **Map...** button in the **Location** area and a map of the world appears from which one can select a desired area anywhere in the world by *picking* the required position on the map (Fig. 15.4). When a spot is *picked* on the map, the Latitude and Longitude show in the appropriate boxes of the dialogue box. These may require precise adjustment when the dialogue box is closed.

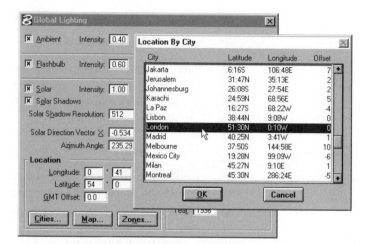

Fig. 15.3 The **Location By City** dialogue box with **London** selected as the required location

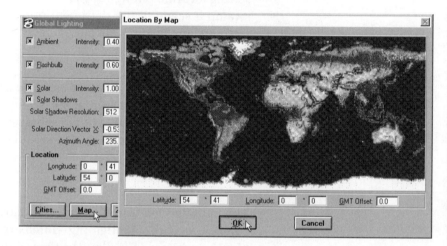

Fig. 15.4 The **Location By Map** dialogue box

Zones

Left-click on the **Zones...** button and a dialogue box appears from which a zone can be selected (Fig. 15.5)

Month, Day and Time

Pick the **P.M** button and a small pop-up list allows selection between a.m. and p.m.

Pick the **Daylight** button and a pop-up list allows a choice between **Daylight** and **Standard** time.

Pick the button currently showing **June** in Fig. 15.2 and a pop-up list appears allowing choice from any month of the year. A figure for the day of the month can be *entered* in the box next to the month button.

The Year can be *entered* in the **Year:** box.

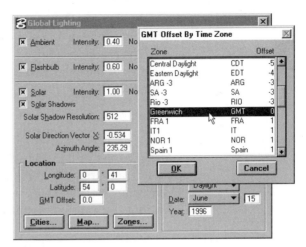

Fig. 15.5 The **GMT Offset By Time Zone** dialogue box

Color

There are three buttons in the dialogue box named **Color....** These are for setting the colours of the ambient lighting, the flashbulb lighting and the solar lighting. A *left-click* on any one of the **Color...** buttons brings up the **Modify Color** dialogue box (Fig. 15.6) from which colours can be selected, either by name from the **Named Colors** lists, or by setting the **Red:**, **Green:** and **Blue:** sliders to mix a required colour.

Solar Shadows

There is a check box in this area of the dialogue box labelled **Lock.** If the Lock check box is on (**X** in check box) then the settings of the **Solar Direction X**, **Y** and **Z vectors** override the settings of the year,

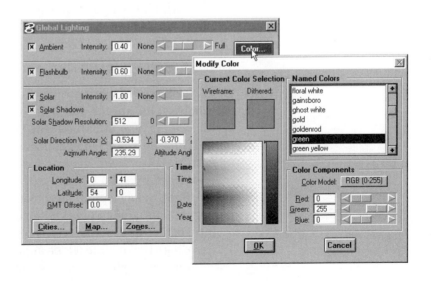

Fig. 15.6 A **Modify Color** dialogue box

month, day and time settings. In fact with the **Lock** check box on, the year, month, day and time settings are greyed out and so cannot be set. The reader is advised to experiment with the X, Y and Z vector settings of the solar shadows to see the effects he/she can obtain by adjusting them.

Source Lighting

Other forms of lighting which can be added to a scene when it is being prepared for rendering are set from the **Source Lighting** dialogue box (Fig. 15.7) called from the **Rendering** sub-menu of the **Settings** pull-down menu (Fig. 15.1).

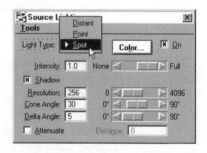

Fig. 15.7 The **Source Lighting** dialogue box

There are three forms of such source lighting as can be seen when the pop-up list from **Light Type:** in the dialogue box is opened – **Distant**, **Point** and **Spot**:

Distant Light: A light of parallel beam which is shed in the direction of the target.

Point Light: A light which radiates in all directions from the point at which the light is placed.

Spot Light: a light in the form of a cone with a central highlighting intensity (the Delta angle of the cone).

To position a source light:

1. In the **Source Lighting** dialogue box set the values required – **Intensity**, **Resolution** and in the case of a **Spot** the cone angles.
2. Choose the type from the **Light Type:** pop-up list.
3. *Left-click* on **Tools** in the dialogue box and select **Place New Light** from the pull-down menu which appears (Fig. 15.8). Lights are positioned by:
   (a) **Spot.** Select a point on screen for the position of the light and *drag* its cone to point to the area of the scene to be targeted.
   (b) **Distant.** Select a point on screen for the position of the light and *drag* a broken line which appears in the direction to the area in the scene where it is to be targeted.

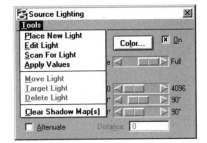

Fig. 15.8 The **Tools** pull-down menu from the **Source Lighting** dialogue box

(c) **Point.** Only its position needs to be located.

It may be necessary to work in two or more view windows to set light positions and targets. To vary their positions or targets select the appropriate tool from the **Tools** pull-down menu.

After placing a light its properties can be seen by using the **Window Area** tool in the scroll bar to zoom right into the area where the light is placed. Figure 15.9 shows these zoomed areas in the case of the three light types.

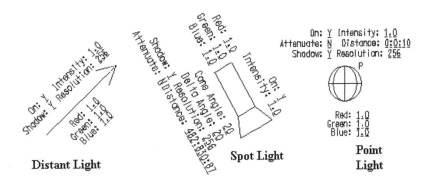

Fig. 15.9 Different types of light source

Distant Light **Spot Light** **Point Light**

The renderings which follow in this chapter are lit from **Ambient**, **Flashbulb** and **Solar** lighting as set in the **Global Lighting** dialogue box. Experimentation with source lights is advised. In order to see the full effects of the placing and targeting of source lights, it is advisable to first turn off Ambient, Flashbulb and Solar lighting in order to see the effects of each source light more clearly. Source lights can be used in conjunction with lighting as set in the **Global Lighting** dialogue box if it is wished to do so to accentuate parts of a scene.

Camera Settings

In the following illustrations a 3D model of a wheel from a trolley will be used to show examples of camera settings. The model is rendered in most of the illustrations with lighting effects taken from the global settings shown in Fig. 15.2 on page 196.

Select the **Camera Settings** tool from the **3D View Control** toolbox (Fig. 15.10). The **Camera Settings** dialogue box appears as shown in Fig. 15.11. To set the camera position, *left-click* in the area to be targeted, then *drag* the cursor away from the target to set the camera position. A broken line square cone appears showing the area covered by the camera.

Fig. 15.10 Selecting **Camera Settings** from the **3D View Control** toolbox

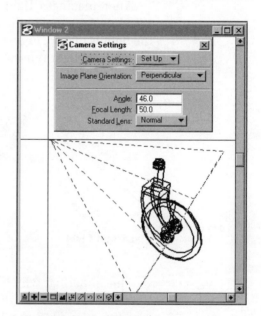

Fig. 15.11 A camera set up with the **Angle** and **Focal Length** at **Normal**

Fig. 15.12 Selecting **Lens** from the **Settings** pull-down menu

Fig. 15.13 **Standard** lens settings from the **Camera Lens** dialogue box

Select **Lens** from the **Camera** sub-menu in the **Settings** pull-down menu (Fig. 15.12). Figure 15.13 shows the settings available from the **Standard Lens** pop-up list in the **Camera Lens** dialogue box which appears.

Different settings of the **Standard Lens** produce results as shown in the series of renderings in Figs 15.14–17.

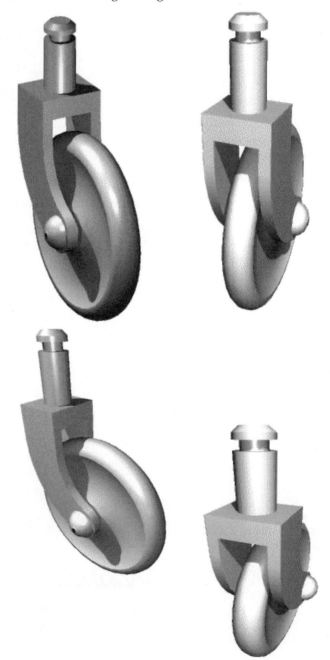

Fig. 15.14 Two views with the camera settings at **Normal**

Fig. 15.15 A view with the camera setting at **Wide Angle**

Fig. 15.16 A view with camera setting at **Extra Wide**

Fig. 15.17 A view with camera setting at **Telephoto**

Other Camera settings

If the **Parallel to Z Axis** setting is selected from the **Camera Settings** dialogue box as shown in Fig. 15.18, the resulting camera angle will be as shown in Fig. 15.18, with the resulting view as shown in Fig. 15.19. Experiment with other settings in the **Image Plane Orientation:** pop-up list in the **Camera Settings** dialogue box.

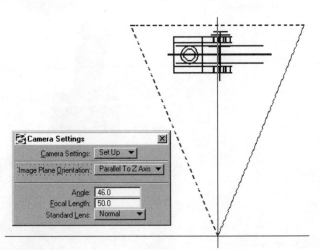

Fig. 15.18 A **Parallel to Z Axis** setting of the camera

Renderings

Select **Render** from the **Utilities** pull-down menu and a sub-menu shows the types of rendering possible in MicroStation 95 (Fig. 15.20). These types differ not only in degree of quality obtained with

Fig. 15.19 The results of the settings given in Fig. 15.18

the type, but in the time taken to perform the rendering. The time depends on the speed of the computer – for example a 66 DX2 Intel computer will take about four times longer to render a given view than a computer fitted with an Intel 120 Pentium. Whatever the computer operating chip, rendering inevitably takes time.

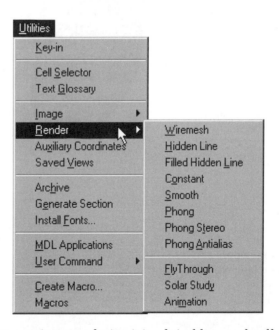

Fig. 15.20 Selecting **Render** from the **Utilities** pull-down menu

Before attempting a rendering it is advisable to make all necessary settings in the **Global Lighting** dialogue box and, if other forms of lighting are also required, set those up as well. The examples of renderings given in this chapter are all with **Global Lighting** settings as shown in Fig. 15.2 on page 196.

Once the lighting conditions have been set, all that is required is to select the type of rendering required from the **Render** sub-menu of the **Utilities** pull-down menu and *left-click* in the view window in which the rendering is to take place.

It is advisable to first render with the **Phong** rendering type. This is not only considerably faster than the **Phong Antialais** type, but will also show whether the lighting effects being sought are suitable. When the rendering is complete if amendments are required in the **Global Lighting** settings, make them and have a second run in **Phong**. Only when satisfied use the best form of shading, which is **Phong Antialias**.

The six illustrations in Figs 15.21–26 give examples of six of the different types of rendering. One not shown, **Phong Stereo**, is only of value with stereo viewing glasses of the red/blue type.

Fig. 15.21 An example of
Wiremesh rendering

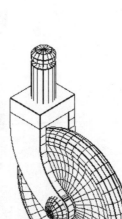

Fig. 15.22 An example of
Filled Hidden Line rendering

Fig. 15.23 An example of
Constant rendering

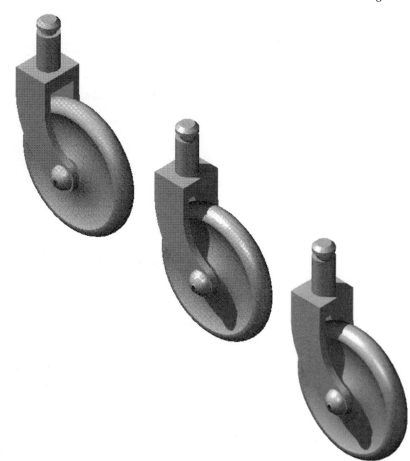

Fig. 15.24 An example of
Smooth rendering

Fig. 15.25 An example of
Phong rendering

Fig. 15.26 An example of
Phong Antialias rendering

Fig. 15.27 Selecting **Saved
Views** from the **Utilities** pull-
down menu

Phong Antialias renders more smoothly than the others. Antialiasing is a mathematical computer method of smoothing outlines in rendered images by amending the shading values in the pixels at the edges of all areas being rendered in order to give the outlines a smooth appearance.

Saving Views

If it is wished to place a view in several orientations, say in the **Isometric View** window, or to zoom part of a model and save that as a view in its own right, then the **Saved Views** dialogue box allows different views to be saved to names *entered* in the dialogue box. To call the dialogue box, select **Saved Views** from the **Utilities** pull-down menu (Fig. 15.27) and the dialogue box appears as shown in Fig. 15.28, in which several views have been saved to different names.

Fig. 15.28 The **Saved Views**
dialogue box

Note

In a saved view the rendering method is not saved, but its orientation
is saved.

MicroStation 95 Masterpiece

Another 'add-on' software package (as was Modeler) which works
inside MicroStation 95 is **Masterpiece**. This is an advanced rendering
programme containing many additional tools.

Materials in renderings

A range of materials can be added to 3D models constructed either
in MicroStation 95 or in Modeler. The files for the materials are held
in palettes in the **materials** directory of the MicroStation 95 directory
(usually **ustation**) with the file extension ***.pal**. The stages involved
in assigning a material to a 3D solid model are given in the following
example:

Stage 1

Select **Render** from the **Settings** pull-down menu and in the sub-
menu which appears select **Assign Materials** (Fig. 15.29). The
Define Materials dialogue box appears (Fig. 15.30).

Fig. 15.29 Selecting **Assign
Materials** from the **Settings**
pull-down menu

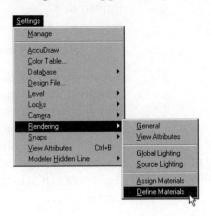

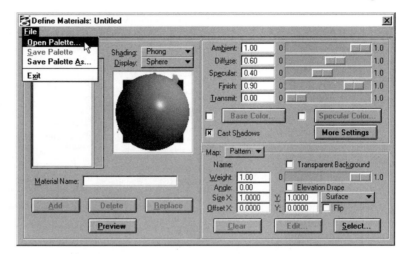

Fig. 15.30 The **Define Materials** dialogue box

Stage 2

Left-click on **File** and in the pull-down menu *pick* **Open Palette...** The **Open Palette File** dialogue box appears (Fig. 15.31). *Double-click* on the filename **metal.pal** and a list of the materials available in the metal.pal file appears in the **Materials:** list box of the **Define Materials** dialogue box (Fig. 15.32).

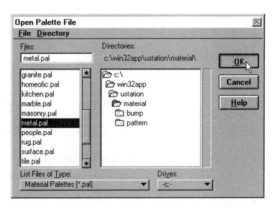

Fig. 15.31 The **Open Palette File** dialogue box

Stage 3

Select the material to be assigned to the 3D model. In this example it is **Brass-polished**. A preview of the appearance of the material comes up in the **Display** area of the dialogue box.

If not satisfied with the appearance of the material showing in the **Display**, some amendments can be made by adjustment of the **Ambient:**, **Diffuse:**, **Specular:** or **Finish** colour sliders, or a **Map** can be added onto the material in a Pattern or a Bump form. In the current

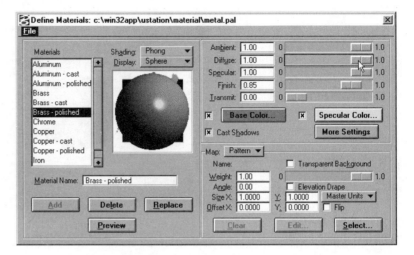

Fig. 15.32 Material files showing in the **Define Materials** dialogue box

example, the **Diffuse:** and **Specular:** lighting sliders have been changed, followed by a *left-click* on the **Replace** button of the dialogue box to replace the original material pattern with the amended one.

Stage 4

Select **Assign Materials** from the **Settings** pull-down menu and in the **Assign Materials** dialogue box which appears, from the **File** pull-down menu select **Open Palette...** (Fig. 15.33). The **Open Palette File** dialogue box appears. In the dialogue box *double-click* on the **metal.pal** filename. A list of the material in the metal.pal file

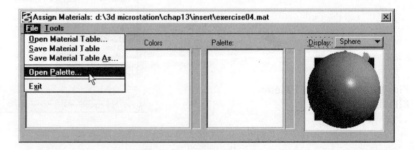

Fig. 15.33 The **Assign Materials** dialogue box

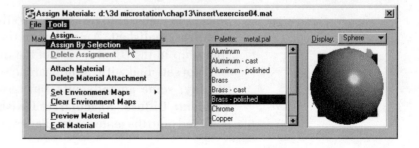

Fig. 15.34 Material names appearing in the **Assign Materials** dialogue box

appears in the **Palette** list of the **Assign Materials** dialogue box (Fig. 15.34).

Stage 5

Double-click on the material name **Brass-polished** in the **Palette** list box. Then select **Assign by Selection** from the **Tools** pull-down menu in the dialogue box and *pick* the 3D model to which the material is to be assigned.

Stage 6

The 3D model can now be rendered as indicated in Fig. 15.35. A colour plate shows this rendering.

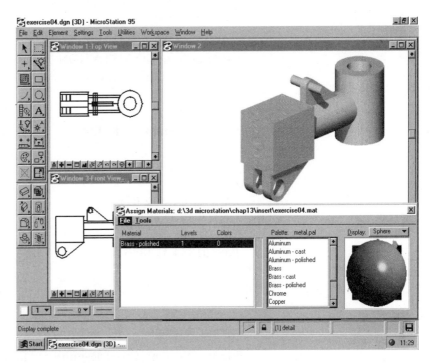

Fig. 15.35 The 3D model has been assigned a material and then rendered

Note

More advanced assigning of materials is available with the rendering program **MicroStation Masterpiece**.

Product information

For more information on the MicroStation family of products and services please contact your nearest Bentley dealer or your nearest Bentley office.

WWW: http://www.bentley.com/
Compuserve: GO MSTATION
e-mail: family@bentley.com

UK

Bentley Systems (UK) Ltd
l'Avenir
Opladen Way
Bracknell
Berkshire RG12 0PF
UNITED KINGDOM
Tel: 01344 412233
Fax: 01344 412386

For further details of the academic edition of MicroStation 95, contact:

3DI Systems
Mill House
Main Street
Hillsborough
Co. Down
NORTHERN IRELAND
Tel: 01846 689217
WWW: http://www.3di.co.uk

Europe

Bentley Systems Czech Republic
Brehova 1
110 00 Praha 1
CZECH REPUBLIC
Tel: (+42) 2 231 6591
Fax: (+42) 2 232 8444

Bentley Systems Finland Oy
Innopoli, Tekniikantie 12
02150 Espoo
FINLAND
Tel: (+358) 04354 3604
Fax: (+358) 04354 3605

Bentley Systems Scandinavia AS
Lyngbyvej 24
DK-2100 Copenhagen
DENMARK
Tel: (+45) 392 71001
Fax: (+45) 392 71041

Bentley Systems France SaRL
CNIT, 2 Place de la Defense
92800 Puteaux
FRANCE
Tel: (+33) 1 46924092
Fax: (+33) 1 46924093

Bentley Systems Germany GmbH
Carl-Zeiss-Ring 3
85737 Ismaning
GERMANY
Tel: (+49) 899 624320
Fax: (+49) 899 6243220

Regerstrasse 5 (for Eastern Europe)
73479 Ellwagen
GERMANY
Tel: (+49) 7965 90050
Fax: (+49) 7965 900520

Bentley Systems Italia Srl
Strada 1, Palazzo WTC
Milanofiori
20090 Assago, Milano
ITALY
Tel: (+39) 257 500254
Fax: (+39) 257 500270

Bentley Systems Europe BV
Polarisavenue 33
2132 JH Hoofddorp
THE NETHERLANDS
Tel: (+31) 23 5685588
Fax: (+31) 23 5685595

Bentley Systems Iberica SA
C/Ochandiano 8
Centro Empresarial el Plantio
28023 Madrid
SPAIN
Tel: (+34) 1 372 8494
Fax: (+34) 1 307 6285

USA

Bentley Systems, Inc.
690 Pennsylvania Drive
Exton PA 19341
USA
Tel: (+1) 610 458 5000
Fax: (+1) 610 458 1060

Asia-Pacific

Bentley Systems Pty Ltd
Suite 8, 51 City Road
South Melbourne VIC 3205
AUSTRALIA
Tel: (+61) 3 9699 8699
Fax: (+61) 3 9699 8677

Far East

Bentley Systems South East Asia
Lot 5.01 5th Floor
Wisma HLA Jalan Raja Chulan
Kuala Lumpur 50200
MALAYSIA
Tel: (+60) 3 242 6233
Fax: (+60) 3 242 7233

Mid-World

Bentley Systems Mid-World Ltd
28 Kennedy Avenue
Suite 401
1087 Nicosia
CYPRUS
Tel: (+357) 2 459936
Fax: (+357) 2 365765

Middle East

Bentley Dubai
PO Box 28149
Dubai
UAE
Tel: (+971) 4 312666
Fax: (+971) 4 312802

Bentley Bahrain
PO Box 10001
Office 32 (Floor 3)
Building 20 Al Khalifa Avenue
305 Manama
BAHRAIN
Tel: (+973) 212 595
Fax: (+973) 214 882

Africa

Bentley South Africa
22 Athlone Road
Parkview 2193
Johannesburg
SOUTH AFRICA
Tel/Fax: (+27) 11 486 0687

Index